LETTERS
from a
SOLDIER
OF FRANCE
1914 - 1915

WARTIME LETTERS FROM FRANCE

WITH AN INTRODUCTION BY
ARTHUR CLUTTON-BROCK

AND A PREFACE BY
ANDRÉ CHEVRILLON

Pen & Sword
MILITARY

This edition published in 2014 by

Pen & Sword Military
An imprint of
Pen & Sword Books Ltd
47 Church Street
Barnsley
South Yorkshire
S70 2AS

This book was first published as 'Letters of a Soldier 1914-15'
by Constable and Company Ltd., 1917.

Copyright © Coda Books Ltd.
Published under licence by Pen & Sword Books Ltd.

ISBN: 9781473823310

A CIP catalogue record for this book is available from the British Library

Printed and bound in England
By CPI Group (UK) Ltd, Croydon, CR0 4YY

Pen & Sword Books Ltd incorporates the imprints of Pen & Sword Aviation, Pen & Sword
Family History, Pen & Sword Maritime, Pen & Sword Military, Pen & Sword Discovery, Pen
& Sword Politics, Pen & Sword Atlas, Pen & Sword Archaeology, Wharncliffe Local History,
Wharncliffe True Crime, Wharncliffe Transport, Pen & Sword Select, Pen & Sword Military
Classics, Leo Cooper, The Praetorian Press, Claymore Press, Remember When, Seaforth
Publishing and Frontline Publishing

For a complete list of Pen & Sword titles please contact
PEN & SWORD BOOKS LIMITED
47 Church Street, Barnsley, South Yorkshire, S70 2AS, England
E-mail: enquiries@pen-and-sword.co.uk
Website: www.pen-and-sword.co.uk

CONTENTS

YOU DO NOT KNOW THE THINGS THAT ARE TAUGHT BY HIM WHO FALLS. I DO KNOW.

(LETTER OF OCTOBER 15, 1914)

INTRODUCTION

I HAVE BEEN ASKED to write an Introduction to these letters; and I do so, in spite of the fact that M. Chevrillon has already written one, because they are stranger to me, an Englishman, than they could be to him a Frenchman; and it seems worth while to warn other English readers of this strangeness. But I would warn them of it only by way of a recommendation. We all hope that after the war there will be a growing intimacy between France and England, that the two countries will be closer to each other than any two countries have ever been before. But if this is to happen we must not be content with admiring each other. Mere admiration will die away; indeed, some part of our present admiration of the French has come from our failure to understand them. There is a surprise in it which they cannot think flattering, and which ought never to have been. Perhaps they also have been surprised by us; for it is certain that we have not known each other, and have been content with those loose general opinions about each other which are the common result of ignorance and indifference.

What we need then is understanding; and these letters will help us to it. They are, as we should have said before the war, very French, that is to say, very unlike what an Englishman would write to his mother, or indeed to any one. Many Englishmen, if they could have read them before the war, would have thought them almost unmanly; yet the writer distinguished himself even in the French army. But perhaps unmanly is too strong a word to be put in the mouth even of an imaginary and stupid Englishman. No one, however stupid, could possibly have supposed that the writer was a coward; but it might have been thought that he was utterly unfitted for war. So the Germans thought that the whole French nation, and indeed every nation but themselves, was unfitted for war, because they alone willed it, and rejoiced in the thought of it. And certainly the French had a greater abhorrence of war even than ourselves; how great one can see in these letters. The writer of them never for a moment tries or pretends to take any pleasure in war. His chief aim in writing is to forget it, to speak of the consolations which he can still draw from the memories of his past peaceful life, and from the peace of the sky and the earth, where it is still unravaged. He is, or was, a painter (one cannot say which, for he is missing), and the moment he has time to write, he thinks of his art again. It would hardly be possible for any Englishman to ignore the war so resolutely, to refuse any kind of consent to it; or, if an Englishman were capable of such refusal, he would probably be a conscientious objector. We must romanticise things to some extent if we are to endure them; we must at least make jokes about them; and that is where the French fail to understand us, like the Germans. If a thing is bad to a Frenchman, it is altogether bad; and he will have no dealings with it. He may have to endure it; but he endures gravely and tensely with a sad Latin dignity, and so it is that this Frenchman endures the war from first to last. For that reason the Germans, after their failure on the Marne, counted on the nervous exhaustion of the French. It was a favourite phrase with them - one of those formulae founded on knowledge without understanding which so often mislead them. - Their formula for us was that we cared for nothing but football and marmalade. - But reading these letters one can understand how they were deceived. The writer of them seems to be always enduring tensely. It is part of his French sincerity never to accept any false consolation. He will not try to believe what he knows to be false, even so that he may endure for the sake of France. Yet he does endure, and all France endures, in a state of mind that would mean weakness in us and utter collapse in the Germans. The war is to him like an incessant noise that he tries to forget while he is writing. He does not write as a matter of duty, and so that his mother may know that he is still living; rather he writes to her so that he may ease a little his desire to talk to her. We are used to French sentiment about the mother; it is a commonplace of French eloquence, and we have often smiled at it as mere sentimental platitude; but in these letters we see a son's love for his mother no longer insisted upon or dressed up in rhetoric, but naked and unconscious, a habit of the mind, a need of the soul, a support even to the weakness of the flesh. Such affection with us is apt to be, if not shamefaced, at least a little off-hand. Often it exists, and is strong; but it is seldom so constant an element in all joy and sorrow. The most loving of English sons would not often rather talk to his mother than to any one else; but one knows that this Frenchman would rather talk to his mother than to any one else, and that he can talk to her more intimately than to any woman or man. One can see that he has had the long habit of talking to her thus, so that now he does it easily and without restraint. He tells her the deepest thoughts of his mind, knowing that she will understand them better than any one else. That foreboding which the mother felt about her baby in Morris's poem has never come true about him:

'Lo, here thy body beginning, O son, and thy soul and thy life,
But how will it be if thou livest and enterest into the strife,
And in love we dwell together when the man is grown in thee,
When thy sweet speech I shall hearken, and yet 'twixt thee and me
Shall rise that wall of distance that round each one doth grow,
And maketh it hard and bitter each other's thought to know?'

This son has lived and entered into the strife indeed; but the wall of distance has not grown round him; and, as we read these letters, we think that no French mother would fear the natural estrangement which that English mother in the poem fears. The foreboding itself seems to belong to a barbaric society in which there is a more animal division of the sexes, in which the male fears to become effeminate if he does not insist upon his masculinity even to his mother. But this Frenchman has left barbarism so far behind that he is not afraid of effeminacy; nor does he need to remind himself that he is a male. There is a philosophy to which this forgetfulness of masculinity is decadence. According to that philosophy, man must remember always that he is an animal, a proud fighting animal like a bull or a cock; and the proudest of all fighting animals, to be admired at a distance by all women unless he condescends to desire them, is the officer. No one could be further from such a philosophy than this Frenchman; he is so far from it that he does not seem even to be aware of its existence. He hardly mentions the Germans and never expresses anger against them. The worst he says of them almost makes one smile at its naive gentleness. 'Unfortunately, contact with the German race has for ever spoilt my opinion of those people.' They are to him merely a nation that does not know how to behave. He reminds one of Talleyrand, who said of Napoleon after one of his rages: 'What a pity that so great a man should have been so badly brought up.' But there was malice in that understatement of Talleyrand's; and there is none in the understatement of this Frenchman. He has no desire for revenge; his only wish is that his duty were done and that he could return home to his art and his mother. To the philosophy I have spoken of that would seem a pitiable state of mind. No one could be less like a Germanic hero than this French artist; and yet the Germans were in error when they counted on an easy victory over him and his like, when they made sure that a conscious barbarism must prevail over an unconscious civilisation.

These letters reveal to us a new type of soldier, a new type of hero, almost a new type of man; one who can be brave without any animal consolations, who can endure without any romantic illusions, and, what is more, one who can have faith without any formal revelation. For there is nothing in the letters more interesting than the religion constantly expressed or implied in them. The writer is not a Catholic. Catholic fervour on its figurative side, he says, will always leave him cold. He finds the fervour of Verlaine almost gross. He seems afraid to give any artistic expression to his own faith, lest he should falsify it by over-expression, lest it should seem to be more accomplished than it is. He will not even try to take delight in it; he is almost fanatically an intellectual ascetic; and yet again and again he affirms a faith which he will hardly consent to specify by uttering the name of God. He is shy about it, as if it might be refuted if it were expressed in any dogmatic terms. So many victories seem to have been won over faith in the modern world that his will not throw down any challenge. If it is to live, it must escape the notice of the vulgar triumphing sceptics, and even of the doubting habits of his own mind. Yet it does live its own humble and hesitating life; and in its hesitations and its humility is its strength. He could not be acclaimed by any eager bishop as a lost sheep returning repentant to the fold; but he is not lost, nor is the universe to him anything but a home and the dear city of God even in the trenches.

His expression of this faith is always vague, tentative, and inconclusive. He is certain of something, but he cannot say what; yet he knows that he is certain, although, if he were to try to express his certainty in any old terms, he would reject it himself. He knows; but he cannot tell us or himself what he knows. There are sentences in which, as M. Chevrillon says, he speaks like an Indian sage; but I do not think that Indian philosophy would have satisfied him, because it is itself satisfied. For he is in this matter of faith a primitive, beginning to build a very small and humble temple out of the ruins of the past. He has no science of theology, nothing but emotions and values, and a trust in them. They are for a reality that he can scarcely express at all; and yet he is the more sure of its existence because of the torment through which he is passing. He uses that word *torment* more than once. The war is to him a martyrdom in which he bears witness to his love, not only for France, but also for that larger country which is the universe. The torment makes him more sure of it than ever before; it heightens his sense of values; and he knows that what matters to a man is not whether he is joyful or sorrowful, but the quality of his joy and his sorrow. There are times when, like an Indian sage, he thinks that all life is contemplation; but this thought is only the last refuge of the spirit against a material storm. He is not one of those who would go into the wilderness and lose themselves in the depths of abstract thought; he is a European, an artist, a lover, one for whom the visible world exists, and to whom the Christian doctrine of love is but the expression of his own experience. For a century or more our world, confident in its strength, its reason, its knowledge, has been undermining that doctrine with every possible heresy. In sheer wilfulness it has tried to empty life of all its values. It has made us ashamed of loving anything; for all love, it has told us, is illusion produced by the will to live, or the will to power, or some other figment of its own perverse thought. And now, as a result of that perversity, the storm breaks upon us when we seem to have stripped ourselves of all shelter against it. The doctrine of the struggle for life becomes a fact in this war; but, if it were true, what creature endowed with reason would find life worth struggling for? Certainly not the writer of these letters. He fought, not only for his country, but to maintain a contrary doctrine; and we see him and a thousand others passing through the fiercest trial of faith at the moment when the mind of man has been by its own perverse activity stripped most bare of faith. So he cannot even express the faith for which he is ready to die; but he is ready to die for it. A few years ago he would have been sneered at for the vagueness of his language, but no one can sneer now. The dead will not spoil the spring, he says No, indeed: for by their death they have brought a new spring of faith into the world.

ARTHUR CLUTTON-BROCK

PREFACE

THE LETTERS THAT follow are those of a young painter who was at the front from September (1914) till the beginning of April (1915); at the latter date he was missing in one of the battles of the Argonne. Are we to speak of him in the present tense or in the past? We know not: since the day when the last mud-stained paper reached them, announcing the attack in which he was to vanish, what a close weight of silence for those who during eight months lived upon these almost daily letters! But for how many women, how many mothers, is a grief like this to-day a common lot!

In the studio and amid the canvases upon which the young man had traced the forms of his dreams, I have seen, piously placed in order on a table, all the little papers written by his hand. A silent presence - I was not then aware what manner of mind had there expressed itself - revisiting this hearth: a mind surely made to travel far abroad and cast its lights upon multitudes of men.

It was the mind of a complete artist, but of a poet as well, that had lurked under the timid reserves of a youth who at thirteen years of age had left school for the studio, and who had taught himself, without help from any other, to translate the thoughts that moved him into such words as the reader will judge of. Here are tenderness of heart, a fervent love of Nature, a mystical sense of her changing moods and of her eternal language: all those things of which the Germans, professing themselves heirs of Goethe and of Beethoven, imagine they have the monopoly, but of which we Frenchmen have the true perception, and which move us in the words written by our young countryman for his most dearly beloved and for himself.

It is singularly touching to find in the spiritual, grave, and religious temper of these letters an affinity to the spirit of many others written from the front. During those weeks, those endless months of winter in the mud or the frost of the trenches, in the daily sight of death, in the thought of that death coming upon them also, closing upon them to seal their eyes for ever, these boys seem to have faced the things of eternity with a deeper insight and a keener feeling, as each one, in the full strength of life and youth, dwelt upon the thought of beholding the world for the last time:

*'Et le monde allait donc mourir
Avec mes yeux, miroir du monde.'*

Solemn thought for the man who has watched through a long night in some advance-post, and who, beyond the grey and silent plain where lurks the enemy, sees a red sun rise yet once more upon the world! 'O splendid sun, I wish I could see you again!' wrote once, on the evening of his advance upon French ground, a young Silesian soldier who fell upon the battlefield of the Marne, and whose Journal has been published. Suddenly breaks in this mysterious cry in the course of methodical German notes on food and drink, stages of the march, blistered feet, the number of villages set on fire. And in how many French letters too have we found it - that abrupt intuition! It is always the same, in many and various words: in those of the agriculturist of the Seine-et-Marne, whom I could name, and who for perhaps the first time in his life takes an interest in the sunset; in those of the young middle-class Parisian who had seemed incapable of speech save in terms of unbelief and burlesque; in those of the artist who utters his emotion in poetry and lifts it up to the heights of stoical philosophy. Through all unlikenesses, in the hearts of all - peasant, citizen, soldier, German schoolmaster - one prevailing thought is revealed; the living man, passing away, feels, at the approach of eternal night, an exaltation of his sense of the splendour of the world. O miracle of things! O divine peace of this plain, of these trees, of these hillsides! And how keenly does the ear listen for this infinite silence! Or we hear of the immensities of night where nothing remains except light and flame: far off, the smouldering of fires; far up, the sparkle of stars, the shapes of constellations, the august order of the universe. Very soon the rattle of machine-guns, the thunder of explosives, the clamour of attack will begin anew; there will again be killing and dying. What a contrast of human fury and eternal serenity! More or less vaguely, and for a brief moment, there comes into passing life a glimpse of the profound relation of the simple things of heaven and earth with the mind of him who contemplates them. Does man then guess that all these things are indeed himself, that his little life and the life of the tree yonder, thrilling in the shiver of dawn, and beckoning to him, are bound together in the flood of universal life?

*   *   *   *   *

For the artist of whom we are now reading, such intuitions and such visions were the delight of long months in the trenches. Under the free sky, in contact with the earth, in face of the peril and the sight of death, life seemed to him to take a sudden and strange expansion. 'From our life in the open air we have gained a freedom of conception, an amplitude of thought, which will for ever make cities horrible to those who survive the war.' Death itself had become a more beautiful and a more simple thing; the death of soldiers on whose dumb shapes he looked with pious eyes, as Nature took them back into her maternal care and mingled them with her earth. Day by day he lived in the thought of eternity. True, he kept a feeling heart for all the horror, and compassion for all the pain; as to his duty, the reader will know how he did that. But, suffering 'all the same,' he took refuge in 'the higher consolations.' 'We must,' he writes to those who love him and whom he labours - with what constant solicitude! - to prepare for the worst, 'we must attain to this - that no catastrophe whatsoever shall have power to cripple our lives, to interrupt them, to set them out of tune... Be happy in this great assurance that I give you - that up till now I have raised my soul to a height where events have had no empire over it.' These are heights upon which, beyond the differences of their teachings and their creeds, all great religious intuitions meet together; upon which illusions are no more, and the soul rejects the pretensions of self, in order to accept what *is*. 'Our sufferings come from our small human patience taking the same direction as our desires, noble though they may be... Do not dwell upon the personality of those who pass away and of those who are left; such things are weighed only in the scales of men. We should gauge in ourselves the enormous value of what is better and greater than humanity.' In truth, death is impotent because it too is illusory, and 'nothing is ever lost.' So this young Frenchman, who has yet never forgone the language of his Christianity, rediscovers amid the terrors of war the stoicism of Marcus Aurelius - that virtue which is 'neither patience nor too great confidence, but a certain faith in the order of all things, a certain power of saying of each trial, "It is well."' And, even beyond stoicism, it is the sublime and antique thought of India that he makes his own, the thought that denies appearances and differences, that reveals to man his separate self and the universe, and teaches him to say of the one, 'I am not *this*,' and of the other, '*that*, I am.' Wonderful encounter of thoughts across the distance of ages and the distance of races! The meditation of this young French soldier, in face of the enemy who is to attack on the morrow, resumes the strange ecstasy in which was rapt the warrior of the *Bhagavad Gita* between two armies coming to the grapple. He, too, sees the turbulence of mankind as a dream that seems to veil the higher order and the Divine unity. He, too, puts his faith in that 'which knows neither birth nor death,' which is 'not born, is indestructible, is not slain when this body is slain.' This is the perpetual life that moves across all the shapes it calls up, striving in each one to rise nearer to light, to knowledge, and to peace. And that aim is a law and a command to every thinking being that he should give himself wholly for the general and final good. Thence comes the grave satisfaction of those who devote themselves, of those who die, in the cause of life, in the thought of a sacrifice not useless. 'Tell —— that if fate strikes down the best, there is no injustice; those who survive will be the better men. You do not know the things that are taught by him who falls. I do know.' And even more complete is the sacrifice when the relinquishment of life, when the renunciation of self, means the sacrifice of what was dearer than self, and would have been a life's joy to serve. There was the 'flag of art, the flag of science,' that the boy loved and had begun to carry - with what a thrill of pride and faith! Let him learn to fall without regrets. 'It is enough for him to know that the flag will yet be carried.'

A simple, a common obedience to the duty at hand is the practical conclusion of that high Indian wisdom when illusions are past. Not to retreat into the solitude, not to retire into the inaction, that he has known and prized; to fight at the side of his brothers, in his own rank, in his own place, with open eyes, without hope of glory or of gain, and because such is the law: this is the commandment of the god to the warrior Arjuna, who had doubted whether he were right in turning away from the Absolute to take part in the evil dream of war. 'The law for each is that he should fulfil the functions determined by his own state and being. Let every man accept action, since he shares in that nature the methods of which make action necessary.' Plainly, it is for Arjuna to bend his bow among the other Kshettryas. The young Frenchman had not doubted. But it will be seen by his letters how, in the horror of carnage, as in the tedious and patient duties of the mine and the trench, he too had kept his eyes upon eternal things.

I would not insist unduly upon this union of thought. He had hardly gained, through a few extracts from the *Ramayana*, a glimpse of the august thought of ancient Asia. Yet, with all the modern shades of ideas, with all the very French precision of form, the soul that is revealed in these letters, like that of Amiel, of Michelet, of Tolstoi, of Shelley, shows certain profound analogies with the tender and mystical genius of the Indies. Strange is that affinity, bearing witness as it does not only to his profound need of the Universal and the Absolute, but to his intuitive sympathy with the whole of life, to his impulses of love for the general soul of fruitfulness and for all its single and multitudinous forms. 'Love' - this is one of the words most often recurring in these letters. Love of the country of battle; love of the plain over which the mornings and the evenings come and go as the emotions come and go over a sensitive face; love of the trees with their almost human gesture - of one tree, steadfast and patient in its wounds, 'like a soldier'; love of the beautiful little living creatures of the fields which, in the silence of earliest morning, play on the edges of the trench; love of all things in heaven and earth - of that tender sky, of that French soil with its clear and severe outlines; love, above all, of those whom he sees in sufferings and in death at his side; love of the good peasants, the mothers who have given their sons, and who hold their peace, dry their tears, and fulfil the tasks of the vineyard and the field; love of those comrades whose misery 'never silenced laughter and song' - 'good men who would have found my fine artistic robes a bad encumbrance in the way of their plain duty'; love of all those simple ones who make up France, and among whom it is good to lose oneself; love of all men living, for it is surely not possible to hate the enemy, human flesh and blood bound to this earth and suffering as we too suffer; love of the dead upon whom he looks, in the impassive beauty, silence, and mystery revealed beneath his meditative eyes.

It is by his close attention to the interior and spiritual significance of things that this painter is proved to be a poet, a religious poet who has sight, in this world, of the essence of being, in ineffable varieties: painter, and poet, and musician also, for in the trenches he lives with Beethoven, Handel, Schumann, Berlioz, carrying in his mind their imaginings and their rhythms, and conceiving also within himself 'the loveliest symphonies fully orchestrated.' Secret riches, intimate powers of consolation and of joy, able, in the gloomiest hours, in the dark and the mud of long nights on guard, to speak closely to the soul, or snatch it suddenly and swiftly to distances and heights. Schumann, Beethoven: between those two immortal spirits that made music for all human ears, and the harsh pedants, the angry protagonists of Germanism, who have succeeded in transforming a people into a war-machine, what likeness is there? Have we not made the genius of those two ours by understanding them as we understand them, and by so taking them into our hearts? Are they not friends of ours? Do they not walk with us in those blessed solitudes wherein our truest self awakens, and where our thoughts flow free?

It is the greatest of all whom a certain group of our soldiers invoke in those days before the expected battle in which some of them are to fall. They are in the depths of a dug-out. 'There, in complete darkness, night was awaited for the chance to get out. But once my fellow non-commissioned officers and I began humming the nine symphonies of Beethoven. I cannot tell what great thrill woke those notes within us.'

That almost sacred song, those heroic inspirations at such a moment - how do they not give the lie to German theories as to the limitations of French sensibility! And what poet of any other race than ours has ever looked upon Nature with more intimate eyes, with a heart more deeply moved, than his whose inner soul is here expressed?

*   *   *   *   *

These letters, despatched day by day from the trench or the billet, follow each other progressively as a poem does, or a song. A whole life unfolds, the life of a soul which we may watch through the monotony of its experiences, overcoming them all, or, again, rapt at the coming of supreme trials (as in February and in April) into perfect peace. It is well that we should trace the spiritual progress of such a dauntless will. No history of an interior life was ever more touching. That will is set to endurance, and terrible at times is the effort to endure; we divine this beneath the simple everyday words of the narrative. Here is an artist and a poet; he had chosen his life, he had planned it, by no means as a life of action. His whole culture, his whole self-discipline, had been directed to the further refining of a keen natural sensibility. Necessarily and intentionally he had turned towards solitude and contemplation. He had known himself to be purely a mirror for the world, tarnishable under the breath of the crowd. But now it was for him to lead a life opposed to his former law, contrary to his plan; and this not of necessity but by a completely voluntary act. That *ego* he had so jealously sheltered, in face of the world yet out of the world, he was now to yield up, to cast without hesitation or regret into the thick of human wars; he was no longer to spend his days apart from the jostling and the shouldering and the breath of troops; he was to bear his part in the mechanism that serves the terrible ends of war. And the close of a life which he would have pronounced, from his former point of view, to be slavery - the close might be speedy death. He had to bring himself to look upon his old life - the life that was lighted by his visions and his hopes, the life that fulfilled his sense of universal existence - as a mere dream, perhaps never to be dreamed again.

That is what he calls 'adapting himself.' And how the word recurs in his letters! It is a word that teaches him where duty lies, a duty of which the difficulty is to be gauged by the difference of the present from the past, of the bygone hope from the present effort. 'In the fulness of productiveness,' he confesses, 'at the hour when life is flowering, a young creature is snatched away, and cast upon a barren soil where all he has cherished fails him. Well, after the first wrench he finds that life has not forsaken him, and sets to work upon the new ungrateful ground. The effort calls for such a concentration of energy as leaves no time for either hopes or fears. And I manage it, except only in moments of rebellion (quickly suppressed) of the thoughts and wishes of the past. But I need my whole strength at times for keeping down the pangs of memory and accepting what is.'

Indeed, strength was called for day by day. This 'adaptation' was no transformation. But by a continuous act of vital energy he assimilated all that he drew from his surroundings. Thus he fed his heart, and kept his own ideals. This was a way to renounce all things, and by renunciation to keep the one thing needful, to remain himself, to live, and not only to live but to flourish; to have a part in that universal life which produces flowers in nature, art and poetry in man. To gain so much, all that was needed was to treasure, unaltered by the terrors of war, a heart eager for all shapes of beauty. For this most religious poet, beauty was that divine spirit which shines more or less clearly in all things, and which raises him who perceives it higher than the accidents of individual existence. And he receives its full influence, and is rid of all anxiety, who is able to bid adieu to the present and the past, to regret nothing, to desire nothing, to receive from the passing moment that influence in its plenitude. 'I accept all from the hands of fate, and I have captured every delight that lurks under cover of every moment.' In this state of simplicity, which is almost a state of grace, he enters into communion with the living reality of the world. 'Let us eat and drink to all that is eternal, for to-morrow we die to all that is of earth.'

That emancipation of the soul is not achieved in a day. The earlier letters are beautiful, but what they teach is learnt by nearly all our soldiers. In these he tells of the spirit of the men, their fire of enthusiasm, their imperious sense of duty, their resolve to carry 'an undefiled conscience as far as their feet may lead.' Yet already he is seeking to maintain control of his own private self amid all the excitement of numbers. And he succeeds. He guards himself, he separates himself, 'as much as possible,' in the midst of his comrades, he keeps his intellectual life intact. Meanwhile he is within barrack walls, or else he is jotting down his letters at a railway station, or else he is in the stages of an interminable journey, 'forty men to a truck.' But to know him completely, wait until you see him within the zone of war, in billets, in the front line, on guard, when he has returned to contact with the very earth. As soon as he breathes open air, his instincts are awake again, the instinct 'to draw all the beauty out,' and - in the shadow where the future hides - 'to draw out the utmost beauty as quickly as may be.' 'I picked flowers in the mud; keep them in remembrance of me,' he will write in a day of foreboding. A most significant trait is this - in the tedium of trench days, or when imminent peril silences the idle tongues, he gathers the greatest number of these magical flowers. In those moments when speech fails, his soul is serene, it has free play, and we hear its own fine sounds. Hitherto we had heard the repetition of the word of courage and of brotherhood uttered by all our gathering armies. But here, in battle, face to face with the eternities, that spirit of his sounds like the chord of an instrument heard for the first time in its originality and its infinite sensibility. Nor are these random notes; they soon make one harmonious sound and acquire a most touching significance, until by daily practice he learns how to abstract himself altogether from the most wretched surroundings. A quite impersonal *ego* seems then to detach itself from the particular *ego* that suffers and is in peril; it looks impartially upon all things, and sees its other self as a passing wave in the tide that a mysterious Intelligence controls. Strange faculty of double existence and of vision! He possesses it in the midst of the very battle in which his active valour gained him the congratulations of his commanding officer. In the furnace in which his flesh may be consumed he looks about him, and next morning he writes, 'Well, it was interesting.' And he adds, 'what I had kept about me of my own individuality was a certain visual perceptiveness that caused me to register the setting of things - a setting that dramatised itself as artistically as in any stage-management. During all these minutes I never relaxed in my resolve to see *how it was*.' He then, too, became aware of the meaning of violence. His tender and meditative nature had always held it in horror. And, perhaps for that very reason, he sought its explanation. It is by violence that an imperfect and provisional state of things is shattered, and what was lax is put into action again. Life is resumed, and a better order becomes possible. Here again we find his acceptance, his submission to the Reason that directs the universe; confidence in what *takes place* - that is his conclusion.

Such times for him are times of observation properly so called, of purer thought in which the impulses of the painter and the poet have no share. That kind of observation is not infrequent with him, when he is dealing with the world and with human action. It awakes at a war-spectacle, at a trait of manners, at the reading of a book, at a recollection of history or art; it is often to the Bible that he turns, and, amid the worst clamours, to the beautiful plastic images of Greece. Admirable is such serene energy of a spirit able to live purely as a spirit. It is admirable, but it is not unique; great intellectual activity is not uncommon with the French; others of our soldiers are philosophers among the shells. What does set these letters in a place apart is something more profound and more organic than thought, and that is sentiment; sentiment in its infinite and indefinite degrees, its relation to the aspects of nature - in a word, that poetic faculty which is akin to the musical, proceeding as they both do from the primitive ground-work of our being, and uniting in the inflexions of rhythm and of song. I have already named Shelley in connexion with the poet we are considering. And it is a Shelleyan union with the most intimate, the most inexpressible things in nature that is revealed in such a note as the following: 'A nameless day, a day without form, yet a day in which the Spring most mysteriously begins to stir. Warm air in the lengthening days; a sudden softening, a weakening of nature.' In describing this atmosphere, this too sudden softness, he uses a word frequent in the vocabulary of Shelley - 'fainting.' In truth, like the great English poet, whom he seems not to have known, he seeks from the beauty of things a faculty of self-forgetfulness in lyrical poetry, an inexpressible and blissful passing of the poet's being into the thing he contemplates. What he makes his own in the course of those weeks, what he remembers afterwards, and what he would recall, never to lose it again, is the culminating moment in which he has achieved self-forgetfulness and reached the ineffable. The simplest of natural objects is able to yield him such a moment; see, for instance, this abrupt intuition: 'I had lapsed from my former sense of the benediction of God, when suddenly the beauty - all the beauty - of a certain tree spoke to my inmost heart; and then I understood that an instant of such contemplation is the whole of life.' And still more continuous, still more vibrant, is at times his emotion, as when the bow draws out to the utmost a long ecstatic tone from a sensitive violin. 'What joy is this perpetual thrill in the heart of Nature! That same horizon of which I had watched the awakening, I saw last night bathe itself in rosy light; and then the full moon went up into a tender sky, fretted by coral and saffron trees.' It is very nearly ecstasy with him in that astonishing Christmas night which no one then at the front can ever forget - a solemn night, a blue night, full of stars and of music, when the order and the divine unity of the universe stood revealed to the eyes of men who, free for a moment from the dream of hatred and of blood, raised one chant along six miles, 'hymns, hymns, from end to end.'

Of the carnage in February there are a few precise notes, sufficient to suggest the increasing horror. The narrative grows quicker; the reader is aware of the pulse and the impetus of action, the imperious summons of duty; the young sergeant is in charge of men, and has to execute terrible tasks. But ever across the tumult and the slaughter, there are moments of recollection and of compassion; and, in the evening of a day of battle, what infinite tranquillity among the dead! At this period there are no more notes of landscape effects; the description is of the war, technical; otherwise the writer's thought is not of earth at all. Once only, towards the end, we find a sorrowful recollection of himself, a profound lamentation at the remembrance of bygone hopes, of bygone work, of the immensity of the sacrifice. 'This war is long, too long for those who had something else to do in the world! Why am I so sacrificed, when so many others, not my equals, are spared? Yet I had something worth doing to do in the world!' Most touching is that sigh, even more touching than the signs of greatness in his soul, for it suddenly breathes an anguish long controlled. It is a human weakness - our own weakness - that is at last confessed, on the eve of a Passion, as in the Divine example. At rare times such a question, in the constant sight of death, in fatigue and weariness, in the long distress of rain and mud, checks in him the impulse of life and of spiritual desire. He was himself the young plant of which he writes, growing, creating fragrance and breaking into flower, sure of God, feeling Him alive within itself. But all at once it knows frost is coming and the threat of unpitying things. What if the universe were void, what if in the infinity of the exterior world there were nothing, across the splendid vision, but an insensate fatality? What if sacrifice itself were also a delusion? 'Dark days have come upon me, and nothingness seems the end of all, whereas all that is in my being had assured me of the plenitude of the universe.' And he asks himself the anxious question, 'Is it even sure that moral effort bears any fruit?' It is something like abandonment by God. But that darkening of his lights passes quickly away. He comes again to the regions of tranquil thought, and leaves them thenceforward only for the work in hand. 'I hope,' he writes, 'that when you think of me you will have in mind all those who have left everything behind, and how their nearest and dearest think of them only in the past, and say of them, "We had once a brother, who, many years ago, withdrew from this world."' How strange is the serenity of these lofty thoughts, how entirely detached from self and from all human things is this spirit of contemplation. Two slight traits give us signs: One night, on a battlefield 'scattered with fragments of men' and with burning dwellings, under a starry sky, he makes his bed in an excavation, and lies there watching the crescent moon, and waits for dawn; now and again a shell bursts, earth falls about him, and then silence returns to the frozen soil: 'I have paid the price, but I have had moments of solitude full of God.' Again, one evening, after five days of horror ('we have no officers left - they all died as brave men'), he suddenly comes upon the body of a friend; 'a white body, splendid under the moon. I lay down near him.' In the quietness, by the side of the dead man, nothing remains but beauty and peace.

*   *   *   *   *

These letters are to be anonymous, at least so long as any hope remains that he who was lost may return. It is enough to know that they were written by a Frenchman who, in love and faith, bore his part in the general effort, the common peril, glad to renounce himself in the pain and the devotion of his countrymen. By a happy fortune that he did not foresee when he left his clean solitude for the sweat, the servitude, and the throng, he no doubt produced the best of himself in these letters; and it may be doubted whether, in the course of a successful artist's life, it would have been given to him to express himself with so much completeness. This is a thought that may strengthen those who love him to accept whatever has come to pass. His soul is here, a more essential soul perhaps, and a more beautiful, than they had known. It was in war that Marcus Aurelius also wrote his thoughts. Possibly the worst is needful for the manifestation of the whole of human greatness. We marvel how the soul can so discover in itself the means to oppose suffering and death. Thus have many of our sons revealed themselves in the day of trial, to the wonder of France, until then unaware of all that she really was. That is how these pages touch us so closely. He who wrote them had attuned himself with his countrymen. Through the more mystical acts of his mind we perceive the sublime message sent to us from the front, more or less explicitly, by others of our brothers and our sons - the high music that goes up still from the whole of France at war. In all his comrades assembled for the great task, he too had recognised the best and the deepest things that his own heart held, and so he speaks of them constantly - especially of the simplest of the men - with so great respect and love. Far from ordinary ambitions and cares, the things that this rough life among the eternities brings into all hearts with a heretofore unknown amplitude are serenity of conscience and a freshness of feeling in perpetual touch with the harmonies of nature. These men do but reflect nature. Since they have renounced themselves and given themselves, all things have become simple for them. They have the transparence of soul and the lights of childhood. 'We spend childish days. We are children.'...

This new youthfulness of heart under the contemned menace of death, this innocence in the daily fulfilment of heroic duty, is assured by a spiritual state akin to sanctity.

ANDRÉ CHEVRILLON

LETTERS OF A SOLDIER

August 6, 1914.

MY VERY DEAR MOTHER, - These are my first days of life at war, full of change, but the fatigue I actually feel is very different from what I foresaw.

I am in a state of great nervous tension because of the want of sleep and exercise. I lead the life of a government clerk. I belong to what is called the depot, I am one of those doing sedentary work, and destined eventually to fill up the gaps in the fighting line.

What we miss is news; there are no longer any papers to be had in this town.

August 13.

We are without news, and so it will be for several days, the censorship being of the most rigorous kind.

Here life is calm. The weather is magnificent, and all breathes quiet and confidence. We think of those who are fighting in the heat, and this thought makes our own situation seem even too good. The spirit among the reservists is excellent.

Sunday, August 16.

To-day a walk along the Marne. Charming weather after a little rain.

A welcome interlude in these troubled times. We are still without news, like you, but we have happily a large stock of patience. I have had some pleasure in the landscape, notwithstanding the invasion of red and blue. These fine men in red and blue have given the best impression of their *moral*. Great levies will be made upon our dépôts, to be endured with fortitude.

August 16 (from a note-book).

The monotony of military life benumbs me, but I don't complain. After nine years these types are to be rediscovered, a little less marked, improved, levelled down. Just now every one is full of grave thoughts because of the news from the East.

The ordinary good-fellowship of the mess has been replaced by a finer solidarity and a praiseworthy attempt at adaptation. One of the advantages of our situation is that we can, as it were, play at being soldiers with the certainty of not wasting our time. All these childish and easy occupations, which are of immediate result and usefulness, bring back calm to the mind and soothe the nerves. Then the great stay which supports the men is a profound, vague feeling of brotherhood which turns all hearts towards those who are fighting. Each one feels that the slight discomfort which he endures is only a feeble tribute to the frightful expense of all energy and all devotedness at the front.

August 25.

This letter will barely precede our own departure. The terrible conflict calls for our presence close to those who are already in the midst of the struggle. I leave you, grandmother and you, with the hope of seeing you again, and the certainty that you will approve of my doing all that seems to me my duty.

Nothing is hopeless, and, above all, nothing has changed our idea of the part we have to play.

Tell all those who love me a little that I think of them. I have no time to write to any one. My health is of the best.

... After such an upheaval we may say that our former life is dead. Dear mother, let us, you and I, with all our courage adapt ourselves to an existence entirely different, however long it may last.

Be very sure that I won't go out of my way to do anything that endangers our happiness, but that I'll try to satisfy my conscience, and yours. Up till now I am without cause for self-reproach, and so I hope to remain.

August 25
(2nd letter).

A second letter to tell you that, instead of our regiment, it was Pierre's that went. I had the joy of seeing him pass in front of me when I was on guard in the town. I accompanied him for a hundred yards, then we said good-bye. I had a feeling that we should meet again.

It is the gravest of hours; the country will not die, but her deliverance will be snatched only at the price of frightful efforts.

Pierre's regiment went covered with flowers, and singing. It was a deep consolation to be together till the end.

It is fine of André[1] to have saved his drowning comrade. We don't realise the reserve of heroism there is in France, and among the young intellectual Parisians.

In regard to our losses, I may tell you that whole divisions have been wiped out. Certain regiments have not an officer left.

As for my state of mind, my first letter will perhaps tell you better what I believe to be my duty. Know that it would be shameful to think for one instant of holding back when the race demands the sacrifice. My only part is to carry an undefiled conscience as far as my feet may lead.

---

1. Second Lieutenant André Cadoux, who died gloriously in battle on April 13, 1915.

MY VERY DEAR MOTHER, - I was made happy by Maurice Barrés's fine article, 'l'Aigle et le Rossignol,' which corresponds in every detail with what I feel.

The dépôts contain some failures, but also men of fine energy, among whom I dare not yet count myself, but with whom I hope to set out. The major had dispensed me from carrying a knapsack, but I carry it for practice and manage quite well.

The only assurance which I can give you concerns my own moral and physical state, which is excellent. The true death would be to live in a conquered country, above all for me, whose art would perish.

I isolate myself as much as I can, and I am really unaffected, from the intellectual point of view. Besides, the atmosphere of the mess is well above that of normal times: the trouble is that the constant moving and changing drags us about from place to place, and growing confidence falters before the perpetually recurring unknown.

August 30.

… My little mother, it is certain that though we did not leave yesterday, it is yet only a question of hours. I won't say to you anything that I have already said, content only that I have from you the approval of which I was certain.

… In the very hard march yesterday only one man fell out, really ill. France will come out of this bad pass.

I can only repeat to you how well I am prepared for all eventualities, and that nothing can undo our twenty-seven years of happiness. I am resolved not to consider myself foredoomed, and I fancy the joy of returning, but I am ready to go to the end of my strength. If you knew the shame I should endure to think that I might have done something more!

In the midst of all this sadness we live through magnificent hours, when the things that used to be most strange take on an august significance.

We have had forty hours of a journey in which the picturesque outdoes even the extreme discomfort. The great problem is sleep, and the solution is not easy when there are forty in a cattle-truck.

The train stops every instant, and we encounter the unhappy refugees. Then the wounded: fine spectacle of patriotism. The English army. The artillery.

We no longer know anything, having no more papers, and we can't trust the rumours which fly among the distraught population.

Splendid weather.

*Saturday, September 5
(at the end of 60 hours in a cattle-truck: 40 men to a truck).*

On the same day we skirted the Seine opposite the forest of Fontainebleau and the banks of the Loire. Saw the château de Blois and the château d'Amboise. Unhappily the darkness prevented us from seeing more. How can I tell you what tender emotions I felt by these magnificent banks of the Loire!

Are you bombarded by the frightful aeroplanes? I think of you in such conditions and above all of poor Grandmother, who indeed had little need to see all this! However, we must hope.

We learn from wounded refugees that in the first days of August mistakes were made in the high command which had terrible consequences. It falls to us now to repair those mistakes.

Masses of English troops arrive. We have crossed numbers of crowded trains.

Well, this war will not have been the mere march-past which many thought, but which I never thought, it would be; but it will have stirred the good in all humanity. I do not speak of the magnificent things which have no immediate connection with the war, - but nothing will be lost.

September 5, 1914
(1st halting-place, 66 hours in the cage without being able to stretch).

Still the same jolting and vibration, but three times after the horrible night there has come the glory of the morning, and all fatigue has disappeared.

We have crossed the French country in several directions, from the rather harsh serenity, full of suggestiveness, of Champagne, to the rich robust placidity of Brittany. On the way we followed the full and noble banks of the Loire, and now...

O my beautiful country, the heart of the world, where lies all that is divine upon earth, what monster sets upon you - a country whose offence is her beauty!

I used to love France with sincere love, which was more than a little *dilettante*; I loved her as an artist, proud to live in the most beautiful of lands; in fact, I loved her rather as a picture might love its frame. It needed this horror to make me know how filial and profound are the ties which bind me to my country...

September 7
(from a note-book).

... We are embarked on the adventure, without any dominant feeling except perhaps a sufficiently calm acceptance of this fatality. But sensibility is kept awake by the sight of the victims, particularly the refugees. Poor people, truly uprooted, or rather, dead leaves in the storm, little souls in great circumstances.

Whole trains of cattle-trucks, which can hardly be said to have changed their use! Trains in which is heaped up the desolation of these people torn from their homes, and how quickly become as beasts! Misery has stripped them of all their human attributes. We take them food and drink, and that is how they become exposed: the man drinks without remembering his wife and children. The woman thinks of her child. But other women take their time, unable to share in the general haste. Among these waifs there is one who assails my heart, - a grandmother of eighty-seven, shaken, tossed about by all these blows, being by turns hoisted into and let down from the rolling cages. So trembling and disabled, so lost...

September 10
(from a note-book).

We arrive in a new part of the country on the track of good news: the strong impression is that France's future is henceforth assured. Everything corroborates this feeling, from the official report which formally announces a complete success down to the most fantastic rumours.

September 13
(from a note-book).

This is war; here are we approaching the place of horror. We have left behind the French villages where peace was still sleeping. Now there is nothing but tumult. And here are direct victims of the war.

The soldiers: blood, mud and dirt. The wounded. Those whom we pass at first are the least suffering - wounds in arms, in hands. In most of them can clearly be seen, in the midst of their fatigue and distress, great relief at having been let off comparatively easily.

Farther on, towards the ambulances, the burying of the dead: there are six, stretched on two waggons. Smoothed out, and covered with rags, they are taken to an open pit at the foot of a Calvary. Some priests conduct, rather than celebrate, the service, military as they have become. A little straw and some holy water over all, and so we pass on. After all, these dead are happy: they are cared-for dead. What can be said of those who lie farther on and who have passed away after nights of the throes of death and abandonment.

... From this agony there will remain to us an immense yearning for pity and brotherhood and goodness.

Wednesday, September 16, 1914.

In the horror-zone.

The rainy twilight shadows the road, and suddenly, in a ditch - the dead! They have dragged themselves here from the battlefield - they are all corrupt now. The coming of darkness makes it difficult to distinguish their nationality, but the same great pity envelops them all. Only one word for them: poor boy! The night for these ignominies - and then again the morning. The day rises upon the swollen bodies of dead horses. In the corner of a wood, carnage, long cold.

One sees only open sacks, ripped nose-bags. Nothing that looks like life remains.

Among them some civilians, whose presence is due to the German proceeding of making French hostages march under our fire.

If these notes should reach any one, may they give rise in an honest heart to horror of the foul crime of those responsible for this war. There will never be enough glory to cover all the blood and all the mud.

War in rain.

It is suffering beyond what can be imagined. Three days and three nights without being able to do anything but tremble and moan, and yet, in spite of all, perfect service must be rendered.

To sleep in a ditch full of water has no equivalent in Dante, but what can be said of the awakening, when one must watch for the moment to kill or to be killed!

Above, the roar of the shells drowns the whistling of the wind. Every instant, firing. Then one crouches in the mud, and despair takes possession of one's soul.

When this torment came to an end I had such a nervous collapse that I wept without knowing why - late, useless tears.

September 25.

Hell in so calm and pastoral a place. The autumnal country pitted and torn by cannon!

September 27.

If, apart from the greater lessons of the war, there are small immediate benefits to be had, the one that means most to me is the contemplation of the night sky. Never has the majesty of the night brought me so much consolation as during this accumulation of trials. Venus, sparkling, is a friend to me...

I am now familiar with the constellations. Some of them make great curves in the sky as if to encircle the throne of God. What glory! And how one evokes the Chaldean shepherds!

O constellations! first alphabet!...

I can say that, as far as the mind goes, I have lived through great days when all vain preoccupations were swept away by a new spirit.

If there should ever be any lapse so that only one of my letters reaches you, may it be one that says how beneficial, how precious have these torments been!

October 1
(from a note-book).

It follows from this that our suffering, every moment of it, should be considered as the most marvellous source of feeling and of progress for the conscience.

I now know into what domain my destiny leads me. No longer towards the proud and illusory region of pure speculation, but in the way of all little daily things - it is there that I must carry the service of an ever-vigilant sensibility.

I see how easily an upright nature may dispense with the arts of expression in order to be helpful in act and in influence. Precious lesson, which will enable me, should I return, to suffer less if fate no longer allows me to paint.

October 9.

It seems that we have the order to attack. I do not want to risk this great event without directing my thoughts to you in the few moments of quiet that are left... Everything here combines to maintain peace in the heart: the beauty of the woods in which we live, the absence of intellectual complications... It is paradoxical, as you say, but the finest moments of my moral life are those that have just gone by...

*   *   *   *   *

Know that there will always be beauty on earth, and that man will never have enough wickedness to suppress it. I have gathered enough of it to store my life. May our destiny allow me time later to bring to fruit all that I have gathered now. It is something that no one can snatch from us, it is treasure of the soul which we have amassed.

October 12.

Up till now your love and Providence do not forsake me... We are still in the magnificent devastated woods, in the midst of the finest autumn. Nature brings many joys which dominate these horrors. Profound and powerful hope, whatever suffering still awaits us.

October 14.

It is true, dear mother, that some renunciation costs a great deal of effort, but be sure that we both possess the necessary strength of soul to live through these difficult hours without catching our breath in painful longing at the idea of the return we both crave for.

The great thing is to know the value of the present moment and to make it yield all that it has of good and beauty and edification. For the rest, no one can guarantee the future, and it would be vain and futile torment to live wondering what might happen to us. Don't you think that life has dispensed us many blessings, and that one of the last, and the greatest, is that we have been able to communicate with each other and to feel our union? There are many unfortunate people here who do not know where their wives and children are, who have been for three months isolated from all. You see that we are still among the lucky ones.

Dear mother, less than ever ought we to despair, for never shall we be more truly convinced that all this agitation and delirium of mankind's are nothing in view of the share of eternity which each one carries within himself, and that all these monstrosities will end in a better future. This war is a kind of cataclysm which succeeds to the old physical upheavals of our globe; but have you not noticed that, in the midst of all this, a little of our soul is gone from us, and that we have lost something of our conviction of a Higher Order? Our sufferings come from our small human patience taking the same direction as our desires, noble though they may be. But as soon as we set ourselves to question things in order to discover their true harmony, we find rest unto our souls. How do we know that this violence and disorder are not leading the universal destinies towards a final good?

Dear mother, still cherishing the firmest and most human hope, I send my deepest love to you and to my beloved grandmother.

Send also all my love to our friends who are in trouble. Help them to bear everything: two crosses are less heavy to carry than one. And confidence in our eternal joy.

October 15, 7 o'clock.

I have received your card of the 1st. What joy it gives me that we should be at last in touch with each other. Certainly, our thoughts have never been apart. You tell me of Marthe's misfortune, and I am happy that you can be useful to her. Dear mother, that is the task that belongs to us both: to be useful at the present moment without reference to the moment that is to follow.

Yes, indeed, I feel deeply with you that I have a mission in life. But one must act in each instant as though that mission was having immediate fulfilment. Do not let us keep back one single small corner of our hearts for our small hopes. We must attain to this - that no catastrophe whatsoever shall have power to cripple our lives, to interrupt them, to set them out of tune. That is the finest work, and it is the work of this moment. The rest, that future which we must not question - you will see, mother dear, what it holds of beauty and goodness and truth. Not one of our faculties must be used in vain, and all useless anxiety is a harmful expense.

Be happy in this great assurance that I give you - that up till now I have raised my soul to a height where events have had no empire over it, and I promise you that my effort will be still to make ready my soul as much as I can.

Tell M—— that if fate strikes down the best, there is no injustice: those who survive will be the better men. Let her accept the sacrifice, knowing that it is not in vain. You do not know the things that are taught by him who falls. I do know.

To him who can read life, present events have broken all habit of thought, but they allow him more glimpses than ever before of eternal beauty and order.

Let us recover from the surprise of this laceration, and adapt ourselves without loss of time to the new state of things which turns us into people as privileged as Socrates and the Christian martyrs and the men of the Revolution. We are learning to despise all in life that is merely temporary, and to delight in that which life so seldom yields: the love of those things that are eternal.

October 16.

We are living for some days in comparative calm; between two storms my company is deserving of special rest. Also I am thoroughly enjoying this month of October. Your fine letter of October 2 reaches me, and I am now full of happiness, and there is profound peace.

Let us continue to arm ourselves with courage, do not let us even speak of patience. Nothing but to accept the present moment with all the treasures which it brings us. That is all there is to do, and it is precisely in this that all the beauty of the world is concentrated. There is something, dear mother, something outside all that we have habitually felt. Apply your courage and your love of me to uncovering this, and laying it bare for others.

This new beauty has no reference to the ideas expressed in the words health, family, country. One perceives it when one distinguishes the share of the eternal which is in everything. But let us cherish this splendid presentiment of ours - that we shall meet again: it will not in any way impede our task. Tell M—— how much I think of her. Alas! her case is not unique. This war has broken many a hope; so, dear mother, let us put our hope there where the war cannot attain to it, in the deep places of our heart, and in the high places of our soul.

October 17, 3 o'clock.

To write to you and to know that my letters reach you is a daily paradise to me. I watch for the hour when it is possible to write.

Yes, beloved mother, you must feel a revival of courage and desire to live; never must a single affection, however good, be counted as a pretext for life. No accident should make us forget the reason we are alive. Of course, we can prefer this or that mission in life, but let us accept the one which presents itself, however surprising or passing it may be. You feel as I do, that happiness is in store for us, but let us not think of it. Let us think of the actions of to-day, of all the sacrifices they imply.

October 22.

I accept all from the hands of fate, and I have captured every delight that lurks under cover of every moment.

Ah! if men only knew how much peace they squander, and how much may be contained in one minute, how far less would they suffer from this seeming violence. No doubt there are extreme torments that I do not yet know, and which perhaps test the soul in a way I do not suspect, but I exert all the strength of my soul to accept each moment and each test. What is necessary is to recognise love and beauty triumphant over violence. No few seasons of hate and grief will have the power to overthrow eternal beauty, and of this beauty we all have an imperishable store.

October 23.

MY VERY DEAR MOTHER, - I have re-read Barré's article, 'l'Aigle et le Rossignol.' It is still as beautiful, but it no longer seems in complete harmony. Now nothing exists outside the absolute present; everything else is like ornaments put to one side until the holiday, the far-off, uncertain holiday. But what does it matter! - the ornaments are treasured up in safety. Thus do I cherish the treasures of affection, of legitimate ambition, of praiseworthy aspiration. All of these I have covered over, and I live but in the present moment.

This morning, under the fine sky, I remembered the music of yesterday: I was full of happiness. Forgive me for not living in an anguish of longing to return. I believe that you approve of my giving back our dearest hopes into other hands than ours.

October 27.

If, as I hope intensely, I have the joy of seeing you again, you will know the miraculous way in which I have been led by Providence. I have only had to bow before a power and a beneficence which surpassed all my proud conceptions.

I can say that God has been within me as I am within God, and I make firm resolves always to feel such a communion.

You see, the thing is to put life to good account, not as we understand it, even in our noblest affections, but in saying to ourselves: Let us eat and drink to all that is eternal, for to-morrow we die to all that is of earth. We acquire an increase of love in that moment when we renounce our mean and anxious hopes.

41

This is nearly the end of the third month of a terrible trial, from which the lessons will be wide and salutary not only to him who will know how to listen, but to all the world, and therein lies the great consolation for those who are involved in this torment. Let it also be the consolation of those whose hopes are with the combatants.

This consolation consists especially in the supernaturally certain conviction that all divine and immortal energy, working through mankind, far from being enfeebled, will, on the contrary, be exalted and more intensely effectual at the end of these storms.

Happy the man who will hear the song of peace as in the 'Pastoral Symphony,' but happy already he who has foreknowledge of it amid the tumult! And what does it matter in the end that this magnificent prophecy is fulfilled in the absence of the prophet! He who has guessed this has gleaned great joy upon earth. We can leave it to a higher being to pronounce if the mission is accomplished.

October 28
(2nd letter, almost at the same hour).

MY DEAR, DEAR MOTHER, - Another welcome moment to spend with you. We can never say any but the same thing, but it is so fine a thing that it can always be said in new ways.

To-day we are living under a sky of great clouds as swift and cold as those of the Dutch landscape painters.

*   *   *   *   *

Dear, I dare not wish for anything - it must not be. I must not even consider a partial relaxation. I assure you that the effort for endurance is less painful than certain times of intensive preparation that we have passed through. Only we can each moment brace ourselves in a kind of resistance against what is evil in us, and leave every door open to the good which comes from without.

... I am glad that you have read Tolstoi: he also took part in war. He judged it; he accepted its teaching. If you can glance at the admirable *War and Peace*, you will find pictures that our situation recalls. It will make you understand the liberty for meditation that is possible to a soldier who desires it.

As to the disability which the soul might be supposed to suffer through the lack of all material well-being, do not believe in it. We lead the life of rabbits on the first day of the season's shooting, and, notwithstanding that, we can enrich our souls in a magnificent way.

October 30.

I write to you in a marvellous landscape of grey autumn lashed by the wind. But for me the wind has always been without sadness, because it brings to me the spirit of the country beyond the hill...

The horrible war does not succeed in tearing us from our intellectual habitation. In spite of moments of overwhelming noise, one more or less recovers oneself. The ordinary course of our present existence gives us a sensibility like that of a raw wound, aware of the least breath. Perhaps after this spoliation of our moral skin a new surface will be formed, and those who return will be for the time brutally insensitive. Never mind: this condition of crisis for the soul cannot remain without profit.

Yesterday we were in a pretty Meuse village, all the more charming incontrast with the surrounding ruins.

I was able to have a shirt washed, and while it dried I talked to the excellent woman who braves death every day to maintain her hearth. She has three sons, all three soldiers, and the news she has of them is already old. One of them passed within a few kilometres of her: his mother knew it and was not able to see him. Another of these Frenchwomen keeps the house of her son-in-law who has six children...

For you, duty lies in acceptance of all and, at the same time, in the most perfect confidence in eternal justice.

Do not dwell upon the personality of those who pass away and of those who are left; such things are weighed only with the scales of men. We must gauge in ourselves the enormous value of what is better and greater than humanity.

Dear mother, absolute confidence. In what? We both already know.

October 30, 10 o'clock.

Up till now I have possessed the wisdom that renounces all, but now I hope for a wisdom that accepts all, turning towards what may be to come. What matter if the trap opens beneath the steps of the runner. True, he does not attain his end, but is he wiser who remains motionless under the pretext that he might fall?

November 1, All Saints', 8 o'clock.

Last night I received your card of 24-25th. While you were looking at that moon, clouded from us, you were very wrong to feel yourself so helpless; how much reason had you to hope! At that very moment I was being protected by Providence in a way that rebukes all pride.

The next day we had the most lovely dawn over the deeply coloured autumn woods in this country where I made my sketches of three years ago; but just here the landscape becomes accentuated and enlarged and acquires a pathetic majesty. How can I tell you the grandeur of the horizon! We are remaining in this magnificent place, and this is All Saints' Day!

At the moment, I write to you in the silvery light of a sun rising over the valley mists; we are conscious of the sleeping country for forty kilometres around, and battle hardly disturbs the religious gravity of the scene.

Do love my proposed picture! It makes a bond with my true career. If it is vouchsafed to me to return, the form of the picture may change, but its essence is contained in the sketch.

Mid-day. - Splendid All Saints' Day profaned by violence.

Glory of the day...

November 2, All Souls'.

Splendid feast of sun and of joy in the glorious beauty of a Meusian landscape. Hope confines itself in the heart, not daring to insult the grief of those for whom this day is perhaps the first day of bereavement.

Dear beloved mother, twenty-eight years ago you were in a state of mourning and hope to-day, the agony is as full of hope as then. It is at a different age that these new trials occur, but a whole life of submission prepares the way to supreme wisdom.

What joy is this perpetual thrill in the heart of Nature! That same horizon of which I had watched the awakening, I saw last night bathe itself in rosy light; then the full moon went up into a tender sky, fretted by coral and saffron trees.

Dear, the frightful record of martyrdom of the best French youth cannot go on indefinitely. It is impossible that the flower of a whole race can disappear.

There must be some nobler task than war for the nation's genius! I have a secret conviction of a better near future. May our courage and our union lead us to this better thing. Hope, hope always! I received grandmother's dear letter and M.R.'s kind and affectionate card.

Dear, have you this beautiful sun to-day? How noble is the country and how good is Nature! To him who listens she says that nothing will ever be lost.

I live only through your thoughts and in the blessings of Nature. This morning our chiefs menaced us with a march of twenty kilometres, and this threat fulfilled itself in the form of a charming walk in the landscape that I love so much.

Exquisite vapours, which we see lifting hour by hour at the call of a temperate sun; and, yonder, those high plateaux which command a vast panorama, where everything is finely drawn, or rather is just felt in the mist...

There are hills furnished with bare trees holding up their charming profiles. I think of the primitives, of their sensitive and conscientious landscapes. What scrupulous majesty, of which the first sight awes with its grandeur, and the detail is profoundly moving!

You see, dear mother, how God dispenses blessings that are far greater than griefs. It is not even a question of patience, since time has no longer any meaning for us, for it is not a matter of any calculable duration. But then, what richness of emotion in each present minute!

This then is our life, of which I wrote to you that not one event must make of it something unachieved, interrupted; and I hope to preserve this wisdom. But at the same time I want to ally it with another wisdom which looks to the future, even if the future is forbidden to us. Yes, let us take all from the hands of the present (and the present brings us so many treasures!), but let us also prepare for the future.

DEAR MOTHER, - Do not hide from me anything of what happens in Paris, of your cares, or your occupations. All that you will decide is for the best. My own happiness, in the midst of all this, lies just in that security I have in thinking of your spirit.

The weather is still exquisite and very soft. To-day, without leaving the beautiful region to which we came on September 20th, we have returned to the woods. I like that less than the wide open view, but there is prettiness here too. And then the sky, now that the leaves have fallen, is so beautiful and so tender.

I have written to C——. I will write to Mme. C——. I hope for a letter from you. If you knew how much the longer is a day without news! It is true I have your old letters, but the new letter has a fragrance which I now can't do without.

November 6.

Yesterday, without knowing why, I was a little sad: what soldiers call *avoir le cafard.* My sadness arose from my having parted the day before with a book of notes which I had decided to send to you in a package. The events of the day before yesterday, albeit pacific, had so hustled me that I was not able to attend to this unfortunate parcel as I should have liked. Also, I was divided between two anxieties: the first, lest the package should not reach you, and lest these notes, which have been my life from the 1st to the 20th of October, should be lost. The second, on the contrary, was lest it should reach you before the arrival of explaining letters, which might seem strange to you, the sending-off having probably been done in another name, and the cover of my copybook bearing my directions that the notes should be forwarded to you if necessary.

*   *   *   *   *

... To-day we are living in the most intimate and delicate Corot landscape.

From the barn where we have established our outpost, I see, first, the road with puddles left by the rain; then some tree-stumps; then, beyond a meadow, a line of willows beside a charming running stream. In the background, a few houses are veiled in a light mist, keeping the delicate darks which our dear landscape-painter felt so nobly.

Such is the peace of this morning. Who would believe that one has but to turn one's head, and there is nothing but conflagration and ruin!...

I have just had your card of the 30th announcing the sending-off of a packet. How kind this is! how much thought is given to us! All this sweetness is appreciated to the full.

Yesterday, a delicious November day. This morning, too much fog for the enjoyment of nature. But yesterday afternoon!

Delicate, refined weather, in which everything is etched as it were on a misty mirror. The bare shrubs, near our post, have been visited by a flock of green birds, with white-bordered wings; the cocks have black heads with a white spot. How can I tell you what it was to hear the solitary sound of their flight in this stillness! - That is one good thing about war: there can be only a certain amount of evil in the world; now, all of this being used by man against man, beasts at any rate are so much the better off - at least the beasts of the wood, our customary victims.

If you could only see the confidence of the little forest animals, such as the field-mice! The other day, from our leafy shelter I watched the movements of these little beasts. They were as pretty as a Japanese print, with the inside of their ears rosy like a shell. And then another time we watched the migration of the cranes: it is a moving thing to hear them cry in the dusk.

* * * * *

... What a happiness to see that you are drawing. Yes, do this for us both. If you knew how I itch to express in paint all our emotions! If you have read my letters of all this time you will know my privation, but also my happiness.

… We have returned to the wide open view that I love so much. Unfortunately we can only catch a glimpse of it through mouse-holes. Well, it is always so!…

… All these days I have been feeling the charm of a country lying in autumn sweetness. This peace was troubled yesterday by the poignant sight of a burning village. It is not the first we have seen, and yet we have not grown used to it.

We had taken up our observation-posts; it was still dark. From our height we saw the tremendous flare and, at daybreak, the charming village, sheltering in the valley, was nothing but smoke. This, in the silvery nimbus of a glorious morning.

From our mouse-trap we had looked to the distance with its prettily winding road, its willow-bordered stream, its Calvary: all this harmony to end in the horror of destruction.

The Germans had set fire to it by hand in the night; they had been dislodged from it after two nights of fierce fighting: their action may be interpreted as an intention to retreat at this point. This proceeding, generally detested by our soldiers, is, I think, forced by strategic necessity. When a village is destroyed it is very difficult for us in the rear to make any kind of use of it. All day we have been witnessing this devastation, while above our heads the little field-mice are taking advantage of the straw in which we are to sleep.

Our existence, as infantry, is a little like that of rabbits in the shooting season. The more knowing of us, at any rate, are perpetually on the look-out for a hole. As soon as we are buried in it, we are ordered not to move again. These wise orders are unfortunately not always given with discrimination; thus, yesterday there were four of us in an advance-trench situated in a magnificent spot and perfectly hidden beneath leaves. We should have been able to delight in the landscape but for the good corporal, who was afraid to allow us even a little enjoyment of life. Later the artillery came up with a tremendous din and showed us the use of these superlative precautions.

None the less, I have been able to enjoy the landscape - alas! a scene of smoke and tragedy yesterday. Be sure, beloved mother, that I do not wish to commit a single imprudence, but certainly this war is the triumph of Fate, of Providence and Destiny.

I pray ardently to deserve the grace of return, but apart from a few moments of only human impatience, I can say that the greater part of my being is given up to resignation.

November 10, 11 o'clock.

MY VERY DEAR MOTHER, - What shall I say to you to-day - a day monotonous with fog. Occupations that are stupefying, not in themselves, but because of the insipid companionship. I fall back on myself. Yesterday I wrote you a long letter, telling you among other things how dear your letters are to me. When I began to write on this sheet I was a little weary and troubled, but now that I am with you I become happy, and I immediately remember whatever good fortune this day has brought me.

This morning the lieutenant sent me to get some wire from headquarters, in a devastated village which we have surrounded for six weeks. I went down through the orchards full of the last fallen plums. A few careless soldiers were gathering them up into baskets. A charming scene, purely pastoral and bucolic, in spite of the red trousers - very faded after three months' campaign…

I am happy in the affection of Ch—— R——. His is a nature according in all its elements with my own. I am sure that he will not be cross with me for not writing, especially if you give a kind message from me to his wife.

The little task confided to me meant walking from nightfall until nine o'clock, but I occasionally lay down in a shelter or in a barn instead of getting back to the trenches for the night.

I do not have good nights of reading now, but sometimes when S—— and I are lying side by side in the trench, you would not believe what a mirage we evoke and what joy we have in stirred-up memories. Ah, how science and intellectual phenomena lead us into a very heaven of legends, and what pleasure I get from the marvellous history of this metal, or that acid! For me the thousand and one nights are renewing themselves. And then at waking, sometimes, the blessing of a dawn. That is the life I have led since the 13th or 14th of October. I ask for nothing, I am content that in such a war we should have relatively a great deal of calm.

You cannot imagine what a consolation it is to know that you give your heart to what concerns me. What pleasure I have in imagining you interested in my books, looking at my engravings!...

November 12, 3 o'clock.

... To-day we have had a march as pleasant as the first one, in weather of great beauty. We saw, in the blue and rosy distance, the far-off peak of the Metz hills, and the immense panorama scattered over with villages, some of which gathered up the morning light, while others were merely suggested.

This is the broad outline of our existence: for three days we stay close to the enemy, living in well-constructed shelters which are improved each time; then we spend three days a little way back; and then three days in billets in a neighbouring village, generally the same. We even gradually form habits - very passing ones, but still, we have a certain amount of contact with the civil population which has been so sorely tried. The woollen things are very effectual and precious.

... We have good people to deal with. The dear woman from whose dwelling I write to you, and with whom I stayed before, wears herself to death to give us a little of what reminds us of home.

But, dear mother, what reminds me of home is here in my heart. It is not eating on plates or sitting on a chair that counts. It is your love, which I feel so near...

Since half-past eight on the evening of the 12th we have been dragged about from place to place in the prospect of our taking part in a violent movement. We left at night, and in the calm of nature my thoughts cleared themselves a little, after the two days in billets during which one becomes a little too material. Our reinforcement went up by stealth. We awaited our orders in a barn, where we slept on the floor. Then we filed into the woods and fields, which the day, breaking through grey, red, and purple clouds, slowly lit up, in surroundings the most romantic and pathetic that could be imagined. In the full daylight of a charming morning we learnt that the troops ahead of us had inflicted enormous losses on the enemy, and had even made a very slight advance. We then returned to our usual posts, and here I am again, beholding once more the splendour of the French country, so touching in this grey, windy, and impassioned November, with sunshine thrown in patches upon infinite horizons.

Dear mother, how beautiful it is, this region of spacious dignity, where all is noble and proportioned, where outlines are so beautifully defined! - the road bordered with trees diminishing towards the frontier, hills, and beyond them misty heights which one guesses to be the German Vosges. There is the scenery, and here is something better than the scenery. There is a Beethoven melody and a piece by Liszt called 'Benediction de Dieu dans la solitude.' Certainly we have no solitude, but if you turn the pages of Albert Samain's poems you will find an aphorism by Villiers de l'Isle-Adam: 'Know that there will always be solitude on earth for those who are worthy of it.' This solitude of a soul that can ignore all that is not in tune with it...

I have had two letters from you, of the 6th and 7th. Perhaps this evening I shall have another. Do not let us allow our courage to be concerned only with the waiting for letters from each other. But the letters are our life, they are what bring us our joys, our happiness, it is through them that we take delight in the sights of this world and of this time.

If your eyes are not strong, that is a reason for not writing, but apart from your health do not by depriving me of letters hold back your heart from me.

November 14
(2nd letter).

DEAR MOTHER WHOM I LOVE, - Here we are again in our usual billet, and my heart is full of thoughts all tending towards you. I cannot tell you all that I feel in every moment, yet how much I should like to share with you the many pleasures that come one by one even in this monotonous life of ours, as a broken thread drops its pearls.

I should like to be able to admire with you this lovely cloud, this stretch of country which so fills us with reverence, to listen with you to the poetry of the wind from beyond the mountain, as when we walked together at Boulogne. But here a great many prosaic occupations prevent me from speaking to you as I feel.

I sent you with my baggage my note-book from August 18 to October 20[2]. These notes were made when we could easily get at our light bags, in the calm of our trench-days, when our danger stopped our chattering, and I could let my heart speak. I found a happiness more intense, wider and fuller, to write to you about. That was a time of paradise for me. But I don't like the billets, because the comfort and the security, relaxing our minds, bring about a great deal of uproar which I don't like. You know how much I have always needed quiet and solitude. Still, I have excellent friends, and the officers are very kind.

But with a little patience and a few thoughts about you I can be happy. How kind this first half of November has been! I have not suffered once from cold. And how lovely it was! That All Saints' Day was nothing but a long hymn - from the night, with its pure moonlight on the dark

---

2. Part of this note-book has already been given.

amber of the autumn trees, to the tender twilight. The immense rosy dream of this misty plain, stretching out towards the near hills... What a song of praise! and many days since then have sung the glory of God. *Coeli ennarrant...*

That is what those days brought to me.

November 15, 7 o'clock.

Yesterday the wild weather, fine to see from the shelter of our billet, brought me apprehensions for to-night's departure, but when I woke the sky was the purest and starriest that one could dream of! How grateful I felt!

What we fear most is the rain, which penetrates through everything when we are without fire or shelter. The cold is nothing - we are armed against it beforehand.

... In spite of all, how much I appreciated the sight of this vast plain upon which we descended, lashed by the great wind. Above the low horizon was the wide grey sky in which, here and there, pale rents recalled the vanished blue. - A black, tragic Calvary in silhouette - then some skeleton trees! What a place! This is where I can think of you, and of my beloved music. To-day I have the atmosphere that I want.

... I should like to define the form of my conviction of better things in the near future, resulting from this war. These events prepare the way to a new life: that of the United States of Europe.

After the conflict, those who will have completely and filiallyfulfilled their obligation to their country will find themselves confronted by duties yet more grave, and the realisation of things that are now impossible. Then will be the time for them to throw their efforts into the future. They must use their energies to wipe out the trace of the shattering contact of nations. The French Revolution, notwithstanding its mistakes, notwithstanding some backsliding in practice, some failure in construction, did none the less establish in man's soul this fine theory of national unity. Well! the horrors of the 1914 war lead to the unity of

Europe, to the unity of the race. This new state will not be established without blows and spoliation and strife for an indefinite time, but without doubt the door is now open towards the new horizon.

To Madame C——.

November 16.

MY DEAR FRIEND, - How much pleasure and comfort your letter gives me, and how your warm friendship sustains my courage!

What you say to me about my mother binds me closer to existence. Thank you for your splendid and constant affection.

... What shall I tell you of my life? Through the weariness and the vicissitudes I am upheld by the contemplation of Nature which for two months has been accumulating the emotion and the pathos of this impassioned season. One of my habitual stations is on the heights which overlook the immense Woevre plain. How beautiful it is! and what a blessing to follow, each hour of the day and evening, the kindling colours of the autumn leaves! This frightful human uproar cannot succeed in troubling the majestic serenity of Nature! There are moments when man seems to go beyond anything that could be imagined; but a soul that is prepared can soon perceive the harmony which overlooks and reconciles all this dissonance. Do not think that I remain insensible to the agony of scenes that we behold all too often: villages wiped out by the artillery that is hurled upon them; smoke by day, light by night; the misery of a flying population under shell-fire. Each instant brings some shock straight to one's heart. That is why I take refuge in this high consolation, because without some discipline of the heart I could not suffer thus and not be undone.

DEAR MOTHER,- ... I write to you in the happiness of the dawn over my dear village. The night, which began with rain, has brought us again a pure and glorious sky. I see once more my distant horizons, my peaked hills, the harmonious lines of my valleys. From this height where I stand who would guess that agricultural and peaceful village to be in reality nothing but a heap of ruins, in which not a house is spared, and in which no human being can survive the hell of artillery!

As I write, the sun falls upon the belfry which I see framed in the still sombre tree close beside me, while far away, beneath the last hills, the last swelling of the ground, the plain begins to reveal its precious detail in the rosy and golden atmosphere.

November 17, 11 o'clock.

The splendid weather is my great consolation. I live rather like an invalid sent to some magnificent country, whom the treatment compels to unpleasant and fatiguing occupations. Between Leysin and the trench where I am at present there has been only uncertainty. Nothing new has happened to our company since October 13.

This is a strange kind of war. It is like that between neighbours on bad terms. Consider that some of the trenches are separated from the enemy by hardly 100 metres, and that the combatants fling projectiles across with their hands: you see that these neighbours make use of violent methods.

As for me, I really live only when I am with you, and when I feel the splendour of the surroundings.

Even in the middle of conversations, I am able to preserve the sensation of solitude of thought which is necessary to me.

November 18.

This morning, daylight showed us a country covered with hoar-frost, a universal whiteness over hills and forest. My little village looks thoroughly chilled.

I had spent the greater part of the night in a warm shelter, and I could have stayed there, thanks to the kindness of my superiors, but I am foolish and timid, and I rejoined my comrades from 1 o'clock till half-past 4.

Curiously enough, we can easily bear the cold: an admirable article of clothing, which nearly all of us possess, is a flour-sack which can be worn, according to the occasion, as a little shoulder-cape, or as a bag for the feet. In either case it is an excellent preserver of heat.

11 o'clock

For the moment there runs in my mind a pretty and touching air by Handel. Also, an allegro from our organ duets: joyful and brilliant music, overflowing with life. Dear Handel! Often he consoles me.

Beethoven comes back only rarely to my mind, but when his music does awake in me, it touches something so vital that it is always as though a hand were drawing aside a curtain from the mystery of the Creation.

Poor dear Great Masters! Shall it be counted a crime against them that they were Germans? How is it possible to think of Schumann as a barbarian?

Yesterday this country recalled to my mind what you played to me ten years ago, the Rheingold: 'Libre etendu sur la hauteur.' But the outlook of our French art had this superiority over the beautiful music of that wretched man - it had composure and clarity and reason. Yes, our French art was never turbid.

As for Wagner, however beautiful his music, and however irresistible and attractive his genius, I believe it would be a less substantial loss to French taste to be deprived of him than of his great classical compatriots.

*   *   *   *   *

I can say with truth that in those moments when the idea of a possible return comes to me, it is never the thought of the comfort or the well-being that preoccupies me. It is something higher and nobler which turns my thoughts towards this form of hope. Can I say that it is even something different from the immense joy of our meeting again? It is rather the hope of taking up again our common effort, our association, of which the aim is the development of our souls, and the best use we can make of them upon earth.

November 19, in the morning.

MY VERY DEAR MOTHER, - To-day I was wakened at dawn by a violent cannonade, unusual at that hour. Just then some of the men came back frozen by a night in the trenches. I got up to fetch them some wood, and then, on the opposite slope of the valley, the fusillade burst out fully. I mounted as high as I could, and I saw the promise of the sun in the pure sky.

Suddenly, from the opposite hill (one of those hills I love so much), I heard an uproar, and shouting: 'Forward! Forward!' It was a bayonet charge. This was my first experience of one - not that I saw anything; the still-dark hour, and, probably, the disposition of the ground, prevented me. But what I heard was enough to give me the feeling of the attack.

Up till then I had never imagined how different is the courage required by this kind of anonymous warfare from the traditional valour in war, as conceived by the civilian. And the clamour of this morning reminds me, in the midst of my calm, that young men, without any personal motive of hate, can and must fling themselves upon those who are waiting to kill them.

But the sun rises over my country. It lightens the valley, and from my height I can see two villages, two ruins, one of which I saw ablaze for three nights. Near to me, two crosses made of white wood… French blood flows in 1914…

From the window near which I write I see the rising sun. It shines upon the hoar-frost, and gradually I discover the beautiful country which is undergoing such horrors. It appears that there were many victims in the bayonet charge which I heard yesterday. Among others, we are without tidings of two sections of the regiment which formed part of our brigade. While these others were working out their destiny, I was on the crest of the most beautiful hill (I was very much exposed also at other times). I saw the daybreak; I was full of emotion in beholding the peace of Nature, and I realised the contrast between the pettiness of human violence and the majesty of the surroundings.

That time of pain for you, from September 9th to October 13th, corresponds exactly with my first phase of war. On September 9th I arrived, and detrained almost within reach of the terrible battle of the Marne, which was in progress 35 kilometres away. On the 12th I rejoined the 106th, and thenceforward led the life of a combatant. On October 13th, as I told you, we left the lovely woods, where the enemy artillery and infantry had done a lot of mischief among us, especially on the 3rd. Our little community lost on that day a heart of gold, a wonderful boy, grown too good to live. On the 4th, an excellent comrade, an architectural student, was wounded fairly severely in the arm, but the news which he has since sent of himself is good. Then until the 13th, terrible day, we lived through some hard times, especially as the danger, real enough, was exaggerated by the feeling of suffocation and of the unknown which hemmed us round in those woods, so fine at any other time.

The important thing is to bear in mind the significance of every moment. The problem is of perpetual urgency. On one side the providential blessing, up till the present, of complete immunity. On the other, the hazards of the future. That is how our wish to do good should be applied to the present moment. There is no satisfaction to be had in questioning the future, but I believe that every effort made now will avail us then. It is a heroic struggle to sustain, but let us count not only on ourselves but on another force so much more powerful than our human means.

November 21.

To-day we lead a *bourgeoise* life, almost too comfortable. The cold keeps us with the extraordinary woman who lodges us whenever we visit the village where we are billeted three days out of nine.

I will not tell you about the pretty view from the window where I write, but I will speak of the interior which shelters many of our days. By day we live in two rooms divided by a glass partition, and, looking through from one room to another, we can admire either the fine fire in the great chimney-place or the magnificent wardrobe and the Meuse beds made of fine old brass. All the delicate life of these two old women (the mother, 87 years old, and the daughter) is completely disorganised by the roughness, the rudeness, the kind hearts and the generosity of the soldiers. These women accept all that comes and are most devoted.

As for Spinoza, whose spirit you already possess, I think that you can go straight to the last theorems. You will be sure to have intuitive understanding of what he says about the soul's repose. Yes, those are moments experienced by us too rarely in our weakness, but they suffice to let us discover in ourselves, through the blows and buffetings of our poor human nature, a certain tendency towards what is permanent and what is final; and we realise the splendid inheritance of divinity to which we are the heirs.

* * * * *

Dear mother, what a happy day I have just spent with you.

There were three of us: we two and the pretty landscape from my window.

Seen from here, winter gives a woolly and muffled air to things. Two clouds, or rather mists, wrap the near hillside without taking any delicacy from the drawing of the shrubs on the crest; the sky is light green. All is filtered. Everything sleeps. This is the time for night-attacks, the cries of the charge, the watch in the trenches. Let our prayers of every moment ask for the end of this state of things. Let us wish for rest for all, a great amends, recompense for all grief and pain and separation.

YOUR SON.

Sunday, November 22, 9.30.

I write to you this morning from my favourite place, without anything having happened since last night that is worth recording - save perhaps the thousand flitting nothings in the landscape. I got up with the sun, which now floods all the space with silver. The cold is still keen, but by piling on our woollen things we get the better of it on these nights in billets. There is only this to say: that to-morrow we go to our trenches in the second line, in the woods that are now thin and monotonous. Of our three stations, that is the one I perhaps like the least, because the sky is exiled behind high branches. It is more a landscape for R——, but flat, and spoilt by the kind of existence that one leads there.

Hostilities seem to be recommencing in our region with a certain amount of energy. This morning we can hear a violent fusillade, a thing very rare in this kind of war, in which attacks are generally made at night, the day being practically reserved for artillery bombardments.

Dear mother, let us put our hope in the strength of soul which will make petition each hour, each minute…

*   *   *   *   *

61

... Yes, it gives me pleasure to tell you about my life; it is a fine life in so many ways. Often, at night, as I walk along the road where my little duty takes me, I am full of happiness to be able thus to communicate with the greatness of Nature, with the sky and its harmonious pattern of stars, with the large and gracious curves of these hills; and though the danger is always present, I think that not only your courage, your consciousness of the eternal, but also your love for me will make you approve of my not stopping perpetually to puzzle over the enigma.

So my present life brings extreme degrees of feeling, which cannot be measured by time. Feeling produced, for instance, by beautiful leafage, the dawn, a delicate landscape, a touching moon. These are all things in which qualities at once fleeting and permanent isolate the human heart from all preoccupations which lead us in these times either to despairing anxiety, or to abject materialism, or again to a cheap optimism, which I wish to replace by the high hope that is common to us all, and which does not rely on human events.

All my tenderness and constant love for grandmother; for you, courage, calm, perfect resignation without effort.

November 23.

DEAR MOTHER, - Here we are arrived in our shelters in the second line. We lodge in earth huts, where the fire smokes us out as much as it warms us. The weather, which during the night was overcast, has given us a charming blue and rosy morning. Unfortunately the woods have less to say to me than the marvellous spaces of our front lines. Still, all is beautiful here.

Yesterday my day was made up of the happiness of writing to you; I went into the village church without being urged by a single romantic feeling nor any desire for comfort from without. My conception of divine harmony did not need to be supported by any outward form, or popular symbol.

Then I had the great good fortune to go with a carriage into the surrounding country. Oh, the marvellous landscape - still of blue and rosy colour, paled by the mist! All this rich and luminous delicacy found definite accents in the abrupt spots made by people scattered about the open. My landscape, always primitive in its precision, now took on a subtlety of nuances, a richness of variety essentially modern.

One moment I recalled the peculiar outer suburbs of Paris with their innumerable notes and their suppressed effects. But here there is more frankness and candour. Here everything was simply rose and blue against a pale grey ground.

My driver, getting into difficulty with his horse, entrusted the whip to me to touch up the animal: I must have looked like a little mechanical toy.

We passed by the Calvaries which keep guard over the Meuse villages, a few trees gathered round the cross.

November 24, 3.30
(back from the march).

I have just received a letter of the 16th and a card, and a dear letter of the 18th. These two last tell me of the arrival of my packet. How glad I am to hear that! For a moment I asked myself whether I was right to send you these impressions, but, between us two, life has never been and can never be anything but a perpetual investigation in the region of eternal truths, fervent attention to the truth each earthly spectacle presents. And so I do not regret sending you those little notes.

My worst sufferings were during the rainy days of September. Those days are a bitter memory to every one. We slept interlocked, face against face, hands crossed, in a deluge of water and mud. It would be impossible to imagine our despair.

To crown all, after these frightful hours, they told us that the enemy was training his machine-guns upon us, and that we must attack him. However, we were relieved; the explosion was violent.

As for my still unwritten verse, *'Soleil si pale,'* etc., it relates to the

11th, 12th, and 13th of October, and, generally, to the time of the battle in the woods, which lasted for our regiment from September 22nd to October 13th. What struck me so much was to see the sun rise upon the victims.

Since then I have written nothing, but for a prayer which I sent you five or six days ago. I composed it while I was on duty on the road.

November 25, in the morning.

... Yesterday, in the course of that march, I lived in a picture by my beloved primitives. Coming out of the wood, as we went down a long road, we had close by us a large farm-house, plumed by a group of bare trees beside a frozen pool.

Then, in the under-perspective so cleverly used by my dear painters with their air of simplicity, a road, unwinding itself, with its slopes and hills, bound in by shrubs, and some solitary trees: all this precise, fine, etched, and yet softened. A little bridge spanning a stream, a man on horseback passing close to the little bridge, carefully silhouetted, and then a little carriage: delicate balance of values, discreet, yet well maintained - all this in front of a horizon of noble woods. A kind of grey weather which has replaced the enchantment, so modern in feeling, of the nuances of last Sunday, takes me back to that incisive consciousness which moves us as a Breughel and the other masters, whose names escape me. Like this, too, the clear and orderly thronging in Albert Duerer backgrounds.

November 26.

DEAREST MOTHER, - I didn't succeed in finishing this letter yesterday. We were very busy. And now to-day it is still dark. From my dug-out, where I have just arrived in the front line, I send you my great love; I am very happy. I feel that the work I am to do in future is taking shape in myself. What does it matter if Providence does not allow me to bring it to light? I have firm hope, and above all I have confidence in eternal justice, however it may surprise our human ideas...

November 28.

The position we occupy is 45 metres away from the enemy. The roads of approach are curious and even picturesque in their harshness, emphasised by the greyness of the weather.

Our troops, having dodged by night the enemy's vigilance, and come up from the valley to the mid-heights where the rising ground protects them from the infantry fire, find shelters hollowed from the side of the hill, burrows where those who are not on guard can have some sleep and the warmth of an Improvised hearth. Then, farther on, just where the landscape becomes magnificent in freedom, expanse, and light, the winding furrow, called the communication trench, begins. Concealed thus, we arrive in the trench, and it is truly a spectacle of war, severe and not without grandeur - this long passage which has a grey sky for ceiling, and in which the floor is covered over with recent snow. Here the last infantry units are stationed - units, generally, of feeble effective. The enemy is not more than a hundred metres away. From there continues the communication trench, more and more deep and winding, in which I feel anew the emotion I always get from contact with newly turned earth. The excavating for the banking-up works stirs something in me: it is as if the energy of this disembowelled earth took hold of me and told me the history of life.

Two or three sappers are at work lengthening the hollows, watched by the Germans who, from point to point, can snipe the insufficiently protected places. At this end the last sentry guards about forty metres.

You can picture the contrast between all this military organisation and the peace that used to reign here. Think what an astonishment it is to me to remember that where I now look the labourer once walked behind his plough, and that the sun, whose glory I contemplate as a prisoner contemplates liberty, shone upon him freely on these heights.

Then, too, when at dusk I come out into the open, what an ecstasy! I won't speak to you of this, for I feel I must be silent about these joys. They must not be exposed: they are birds that love silence... Let us confine our speech to that essential happiness which is not easily affrighted - the happiness of feeling ourselves prepared equally for all.

November 29, in the morning
(from a billet).

MY VERY DEAR MOTHER, - Yesterday evening I left the first line trenches in broken weather which, in the night, after my arrival here, turned into rain. I watch it falling through the fog from my favourite window. If you like I will tell you of the wonders I saw yesterday.

From the position described in my letter of yesterday, can be seen, as I have often written to you, the most marvellous horizon. Yesterday a terrible wind rent a low veil of clouds which grew red at their summits. Perhaps the background of my 'Haheyna' will give you a faint idea of what it was. But how much more majestic and full of animation was the emotion I experienced yesterday.

The hills and valleys passed in turn from light to shade, now defined, now veiled, according to the movement of the mists. High up, blue spaces fringed with light.

Such was the beauty of yesterday. Shall I speak of the evenings that went before, when, on my way along the road, the moon brought out the pattern of the trees, the pathetic Calvaries, the touching spectacle of houses which one knew were ruins, but which night seemed to make stand forth again like an appeal for peace.

I am glad to see you like Verlaine. Read the fine preface by Coppee to the selected works, which you will find in my library.

His fervour has a spontaneity, I might almost say a grossness, which always repels me a little, just because it belongs to that kind of Catholic fervour which on its figurative side will always leave me cold. But what a poet!

He has been my almost daily delight both here and when I was in Paris; often the music of his *Paysages Tristes* comes back to me, exactly expressing the emotion of certain hours. His life is as touching as that of a sick animal, and one almost wonders that a like indignity has not withered the exquisite flowers of his poetry. His conversion, that of an artist rather than of a thinker, followed on a great upsetting of his existence which resulted from grave faults of his. (He was in prison.)

In the *Lys Rouge* Anatole France has drawn a striking portrait of him, under the name of Choulette; perhaps you will find we have this book.

In *Sagesse* the poems are fine and striking because of the true impulse and sincerity of the remorse. A little as though the cry of the *Nuit de Mai* resounded all through his work.

Our two great poets of the last century, Musset and Verlaine, were two unhappy beings without any moral principle with which to stake up their flowers of thought - yet what magnificent and intoxicating flowers.

Perhaps I tire you when I speak thus on random subjects, but to do so enables me to plunge back into my old life for a little while. Since I had the happiness of getting your letters, I have not taken note of anything. Do not think that distractions by the way make me forgetful of our need and hope, but I believe it is just the beautiful adornment of life which gives it, for you and me, its value.

I am still expecting letters from you after that of the 22nd, but I am sure to get them here in this billet. Thank you for the parcel you promise: poor mothers, what pains they all take!

December 1, in the morning
(from a billet).

I remember the satisfaction I felt in my freedom when I was exempted from my military duties. It seemed to me that if, at twenty-seven years old, I had been obliged to return to the regiment, my life and career would have been irretrievably lost. And here I am now, twenty-eight years old, back in the army, far from my work, my responsibilities, my ambitions - and yet never has life brought me such a full measure of finer feelings; never have I been able to record such freshness of sensibility, such security of conscience. So those are the blessings arising out of the thing which my reasonable human foresight envisaged as disaster. And thus continues the lesson of Providence which, upsetting all my fears, makes good arise out of every change of situation.

The two last sunrises, yesterday and to-day, were lovely…

I feel inclined to make you a little sketch of the view from my window…

* * * * *

It is done from memory; in your imagination you must add streaks of purple colour, making the most dramatic effect, and an infinite stretch of open country to right and left. This is what I have been able again and again to look upon, during this time. At this moment, the soft sky brings into harmony the orchards where we work. My little job dispenses me from digging for the time. Such are the happinesses which, from afar, had the appearance of calamities.

December 1
(2nd letter).

I have just received your letters of the 25th, 26th, and 27th, as well as a dear letter from Grandmother, so valiant, so full of spirit, and so clear-minded. It gave me great pleasure, and brings me a dear hope, of which I accept the augury with joy. Each one of your beloved letters, too, gives me the best of what life holds for me. My first letter of to-day replies to what you say about the acceptation of trials and the destruction of idols.

You will see that I think absolutely as you do, and I trust that there is in this hour no impeding idol in my heart…

I think that my last prayer is in fact very simple. The spirit of the place could not have borne to be clothed in an art that was overloaded. God was everywhere, and everywhere was harmony: the road at night, of which I speak to you so often, the starry sky, the valley full of the murmuring of water, the trees, the Calvaries, the hills near and far. There would not have been any room for artifice. It is useless for me to give up being an artist, but I hope always to be sincere and to use art as it were only for the clothing of my conscience.

December 5, in the morning.

… We have come out of our burrows, and three days of imprisonment are followed by a morning in the open. It would be impossible to imagine such a state of mud.

Your pretty aluminium watch is the admiration of everybody.

Is André's wound serious? The mothers endure terrible agony in this war, but courage - nothing will be lost. As for me, I get on all right, and am as happy as one may be.

A terrific wind to-day, chasing the fine clouds. Keen air, in which the branches thrive. Beautiful moonlight on all these nights, all the more appreciated if one has been cheated of the day.

Dear, I am writing badly to-day because we are bewildered by the full daylight after those long hours of darkness, but my heart goes out to you and rests with you.

… Let us bring to everything the spirit of courage. Let us have confidence in God always, whatever happens. How much I feel, as you do, that one can adore Him only with one's spirit! And like you I think that we must avoid all pride which condemns the ways of other people. Let our love lead us in union towards the universal Providence. Let us, in constant prayer, give back our destiny into His hands. Let us humbly admit to Him our human hopes, trying at every moment to link them to eternal wisdom. It is a task which now seems full of difficulty, but difficulty is in everything in life.

Sunday, December 6.

I am happy to see you so determinedly courageous. We have need of courage, or, rather, we have need of something difficult to obtain, which is neither patience nor overconfidence, but a certain belief in the order of things, the power to be able to say of every trial that it is well.

Our instinct for life makes us try to free ourselves from our obligations when they are too cruel, too oft-repeated, but, as I am happy to know, you have been able to see what Spinoza understood by human liberty. Inaccessible ideal, to which one must cling nevertheless…

… Dear mother, these trials that we must accept are long, but notwithstanding their unchanging form one cannot call them monotonous, since they call upon courage which must be perpetually new. Let us unite together for God to grant us strength and resource in accepting everything…

You know what I call religion: that which unites in man all his ideas of the universal and the eternal, those two forms of God. Religion, in the ordinary sense of the word, is but the binding together of certain moral and disciplinary formulas with the fine poetic imagery of the great biblical and Christian philosophies.

Do not let us offend any one. Looked at properly, religious formulas, however apart they may remain from my own habit of mind, seem to me praiseworthy and sympathetic in all that they contain of aspiration and beauty and form.

Dear mother whom I love, let us always hope: trials are legion, but beauty remains. Let us pray that we may long continue to contemplate it…

Monday, December 7.

MY BELOVED MOTHER, - I am writing this in the night . . . by six o'clock in the morning military life will be in full swing.

My candle is stuck on a bayonet, and every now and then a drop of water falls on to my nose. My poor companions try to light a reluctant fire. Our time in the trenches transforms us into lumps of mud.

The general good humour is admirable. However the men may long to return, they accept none the less heroically the vicissitudes of the situation. Their courage, infinitely less 'literary' than mine, is so much the more practical and adaptable; but each bird has its cry, and mine has never been a war-cry. I am happy to have felt myself responsive to all these blows, and my hope lies in the thought that they will have forged my soul. Also I place confidence in God and whatever He holds in store for me.

I seem to foresee my work in the future. Not that I build much on this presentiment, for all artists have conceived work which has never come to light. Mozart was about to make a new start when he died, and Beethoven planned the 'Tenth Symphony' in ignorance of the all too brief time that was to be allowed him by destiny.

It is the duty of the artist to open his flowers without dread of frost, and perhaps God will allow my efforts to fulfil themselves in the future. My very various attempts at work all have an indescribable immaturity about them still, a halting execution, which consorts badly with the real loftiness of the intention. It seems to me that my art will not quite expand until my life is further advanced. Let us pray that God will allow me to attain...

As for what is in your own heart, I have such confidence in your courage that this certainty is my great comfort in this hour. I know that my mother has gained that freedom of soul which allows contemplation of the universal scheme of things. I know from my own experience how intermittent is this wisdom, but even to taste of it is already to possess God. It is the security I derive from knowledge of your soul and your love, that enables me to think of the future in whatever form it may come.

December 9.

DEAR MOTHER, - P—— L——, in his charming letter, tells me he would willingly exchange his philosophers for a gun. He is quite wrong. For one thing, Spinoza is a most valuable aid in the trenches; and then it is those who are still in a position to profit by culture and progress who must now carry on French thought. They have an overwhelmingly difficult task, calling for far more initiative than ours. We are free of all burden. I think our existence is like that of the early monks: hard, regular discipline and freedom from all external obligations.

December 10
(a marvellous morning).

Our third day in billets brings us the sweetness of friendly weather. The inveterate deluge of our time in the first line relents a little,and the sun shows itself timidly.

Our situation, which has been pleasant enough during the last twomonths, may now be expected entirely to change.

The impregnability of the positions threatens to make the war interminable; one of the two adversaries must use his offensive to unlock the situation and precipitate events. I think the high command faces this probability - and I hardly dare tell you that I cannot regret anything that increases the danger.

Our life, of which a third part is flatly *bourgeois* and the two other parts present just about the same dangers as, say, chemical works do, will end by deadening all sensibility. It is true we shall be grieved to leave what we are used to, but perhaps we were getting too accustomed to a state of well-being which could not last.

My own circumstances are perhaps going to change. I shall probably lose my course, being mentioned for promotion to the rank of corporal, which means being constantly in the trenches and various duties in the first line. I hope God will continue to bless me.

... I feel that we have nothing to ask. If there should be in us something eternal which we must still manifest on earth, we may be sure that God will let us do it.

December 10
(2nd letter).

Happily you and I live in a domain where everything unites us without our having to write our thoughts...

The weather is overcast again and promises us a wet time in the first and second lines.

The day declines, and a great melancholy falls too upon everything. This is the hour of sadness for those who are far away, for all the soldiers whose hearts are with their homes, and who see night closing down upon the earth.

I come to you, and immediately my heart grows warm. I can feel your attentive tenderness, and the wisdom which inspires your courage. Sometimes I am afraid of always saying the same thing, but how can I find new words for my poor love, tossed always through the same vicissitudes? Now that we are going to set out, perhaps we shall have to leave behind many cherished keepsakes, but the soul should not be strongly tied to fetiches. We are fond of clinging to many things, but love can do without them.

December 12, 10 o'clock
(card).

A soft day under the rain. All goes well in our melancholy woods. In various parts of the neighbourhood there has been a terrible cannonade.

Received your letters of the 4th and 6th. They brought me happiness: they are the true joy of life. I am glad you visited C——. I hope to write to you at greater length. It is not that I have less leisure than usual, but I am going through a time when I am less sensible to the beauty of things. I long for true wisdom…

To-day, in spite of the changing beauty of sun and rain, I did not feel alive to Nature. Yet never was there such grace and goodness in the skies.

The landscape, with the little bridge and the man on horseback of which I have told you, softened under the splendour of the clouds. But I had lapsed from my former sense of the benediction of God, when suddenly the beauty, all the beauty, of a certain tree spoke to my inmost heart. It told me of fairness that never fails; of the greenness of ivy and the redness of autumn, the rigidity of winter in the branches; - and then I understood that an instant of such contemplation is the whole of life, the very reward of existence, beside which all human expectation is nothing but a bad dream.

Sunday, December 13.

… After a refreshing night I walked to-day in these woods where for three months the dead have strewn the ground. To-day the vanishing autumn displayed its richness, and the same beauty of mossy trunks spoke to me, as it did yesterday, of eternal joy.

I am sure it needs an enormous effort to feel all this, but it must be felt if we are to understand how little the general harmony is disturbed by that which intolerably assails our emotions.

We must feel that all human uprooting is only a little thing, and what is truly ourselves is the life of the soul.

We are still here in the region of the first line, but in a place where we can lift our heads and behold the charm of my Meusian hills, clearing in the delicate weather.

Above the village and the orchards I see the lines of birches and firs. Some have their skeletons coloured with a diaphanous violet marked with white. Others build up the horizon with stronger lines.

I have been strengthened by the splendid lesson given me by a beautiful tree during a march. Ah, dear mother, we may all disappear and Nature will remain, and the gift I had from her of a moment of herself is enough to justify a whole existence. That tree was like a soldier.

You would not believe how much harm has been done to the forests about here: it is not so much the machine-guns as the frightful amount of cutting necessary for making our shelters and for our fuel. Ah well, in the midst of this devastation something told me that there will always be beauty, in man and in tree.

For man also gives this lesson, though in him it is less easily distinguished: it is a fine thing to see the splendid vitality of all this youth, whose force no harvest can diminish.

December 15, morning.

I have had your dear letter of the 9th, in which you speak of our home. It makes me happy to feel how fine and strong is the force of life which soon adjusts itself to each separation and uprooting. It makes me happy, too, to think that my letters find an echo in your heart. Sometimes I was afraid of boring you, because though our life is so fine in many ways, it is certainly very primitive, and there are not many salient things to relate.

If only I could follow my calling of painter I could have recourse to these wonderful visions that lie before me, and I could find vent for all

75

the pent-up artist's emotion that is within me. As it is, in trying to speak of the sky, the tree, the hill, or the horizon, I cannot use words as subtle as they, and the infinite variety of these things can only be named in the same general terms, which I am afraid of constantly repeating...

December 15.

One must adapt oneself to this special kind of life, which is indigent as far as intellectual activity goes, but marvellously rich in emotion. I suppose that in troubled times for many centuries there have been men who, weary of luxury, have sought in the peace of the cloister the contemplation of eternal things; contemplation threatened by the crowd, but a refuge even so. And so I think our life is like that of the monks of old, who were military too, and more apt at fighting than I could ever be. Among them, those who willed could know the joy which I now find.

To-day I have a touching letter from Madame M——, whose spirit I love and admire.

Changeable but very beautiful weather.

It is impossible to say more than we have already said about the attitude we must adopt in regard to events. The important thing is to put this attitude in practice. It is not easy, as I have learnt in these last days, though no new difficulty had arisen to impede my path towards wisdom.

... Tormenting anxiety can sometimes be mistaken for an alert conscience.

December 16.

Yesterday in our shelter I got out your little album - very much damaged, alas - and I tried to copy some of the lines of the landscape. I was stopped by the cold, and I was returning dissatisfied when I suddenly had the idea of making one of my friends sit for me. How can I tell you what a joy it was to get a good result! I believe that my little pencil proved entirely successful. The sketch has been sent away in a letter to some friend of his. It was such a true joy to me to feel I had not lost my faculty.

December 17
(in a new billet).

… Last night we left behind all that was familiar when we came out of the first-line trenches after three days of perfect peace there. We were told off to the billet which we occupied on October 6th and 7th. One can feel in the air the wind of change. I don't know what may come, but the serenity of the weather to-day seems an augury of happiness.

These have been days of marvellous scenes, which I can appreciate better now than during those few days of discouragement, which came because I allowed myself to reckon things according to our miserable human standards.

I write to you by a window from which I watch the sunset. You see that goodness is everywhere for us.

3 o'clock.

… I take up this letter once more in the twilight of an exceptional winter: the day fades away as calmly as it came. I am watching the women washing clothes under the lines of trees on the river bank; there is peace everywhere - I think even in our hearts. Night falls…

A sweet day, ending here round the table. Quiet, drawing, music. I can think with calm of the length of the days to come when I realise how swift have been these days that are past. Half the month is gone, and Christmas comes in the midst of war. The only thing for me is to adapt myself entirely to these conditions of existence, and, owing to my union with you, to gain a degree of acceptance which is of an order higher than human courage.

December 21, morning.

MY VERY DEAR MOTHER, - I have told you freely in my letters of my happiness; but the rock ahead of happiness is that poor humanity is in perpetual fear of losing it. In spite of all experience, we do not realise that in the eternal scheme of things a new happiness always grows at the side of an old one.

For myself, I have not to look for a new one. I have only to try to reconcile two wisdoms. One, which is human, prompts me to cultivate my happiness, but the other teaches me that human happiness is a most perishable flower.

We may say: Let us make use of the joys chosen by an upright conscience; but let us never forget how swiftly these pass.

Yes, the Holy Scriptures contain the finest and most poetical philosophy. I think they owe it to their affiliation to the oldest philosophies. There are many disputable things in Edouard Schure, but what remains is the divination which made him climb through all doctrine to the infinitely distant Source of human wisdom.

Do you know that those touching traditions of the Good Shepherd and the Divine Mother, so happily employed in our Christian religions, are the creations of the oldest symbolism? The Greeks derived them from their own spiritual ancestors; with them the good shepherd was called Hermes, the god of the migration of souls. In the same way, the type of our Madonna is the great Demeter, the mother who bears an infant in her arms.

One feels that all religions, as they succeeded each other, transmitted the same body of symbols, renewed each time by humanity's perpetually-young spirit of poetry.

December 23
(in the dark).

I had begun this letter yesterday, when I was forced to leave off. It was then splendid weather, which has lasted fairly well. But we are now back again in our first lines. This time we are occupying the village itself, our pretty Corot village of two months ago. But our outpost is situated in a house where we are obliged to show no sign of life, so as to conceal our presence from the enemy. And so here we are at nine o'clock in the morning, in a darkness that would make it seem to be late on Christmas eve.

Your dear letter lately received has given me great joy. It is true that Grace and Inspiration are two names for the same thing.

If you are going to see the pictures of the great poet Gustave Moreau, you will see a panel called *La vie de l'humanité* (I believe). It consists of nine sections in three divisions, called *l'Age d'or, l'Age d'argent, l'Age de fer.* Above is a pediment from which Christ presides over this human panorama. But this is where this great genius has the same intuition as you had: each of the three parts bears the name of a hero - Adam, Orpheus, and Cain, and each one represents three periods. Now, the periods of the golden age are called Ecstasy, Prayer, and Sleep, while the periods of the silver age are called Inspiration, Song, and Tears.

Ecstasy is the same as Grace, because the picture shows Adam and Eve in the purity of their souls, in a scene of flowers, and in the enjoyment of divine contemplation. The harmony of Nature itself urges them on in their impulse towards God.

In the silver age, Inspiration is still Grace, but just beginning to be complicated by human artifice. The poet Orpheus perpetually contemplates God, but the Muse is always at his elbow, the symbol of human art is already born; and that great human manifestation of God, Song, brings with it grief and tears.

Following out the cycle and coming to human evil, Gustave Moreau shows the iron age - Cain condemned to labour and sorrow.

This work shows that the divine moment may be seized, but is fugitive and can never remain with man. It explains our failures. People say that the picture is too literary, but it touches the heart of those who wish to break through the ice with which all human expression is chilled.

Undoubtedly Rembrandt was the Poet of genius *par excellence*, at the same time as he was pure Painter. But let us grant that ours is a less rich time, our temperaments less universal; and let us recognise the beauty of Gustave Moreau's poem, of which, in two words, you expressed the spirit.

YOUR SON.

December 24, morning.

Our first day in the outpost passed away in the calm of a country awaiting snow. It came in the night.

In the back gardens, which lie in sight of the Germans, I went out to see it, where it emphasised and ennobled the least of things. Then I came back to my candle, and I write on a table where my neighbour is grating chocolate. So that is war.

Military life has some amusing surprises. We had to come to the first line before two non-commissioned officers found a bath and could bathe themselves. As for me, I have made myself a water-jug out of a part of a 75.

... I will not speak of patience, since a reserve of mere patience may be useless preparation for the unknown quantity. But I must say that the time goes extremely quickly.

We spend child-like days; indeed we are children in regard to these events, and the benefit of this war will have been to restore youth to the hearts of those who return.

Dear mother, our village has just had a visit from two shells. Will they be followed by others? May God help us! The other day they sent us a hundred and fifteen, to wound one man in the wrist!

A house in which a section of our company is living is in flames. We have not seen a soul stirring. We can only hope that it is well with them.

I am deeply happy to have lived through these few months. They have taught me what one can make of one's life, in any circumstances.

My fellow-soldiers are splendid examples of the French spirit… They swagger, but their swagger is only the outer form of a deep and magnificent courage.

My great fault as an artist is that I am always wanting to clothe the soul of the race in some beautiful garment painted in my own colours. And when people irritate me it is that they are soiling these beautiful robes; but, as a matter of fact, they would find them a bad encumbrance in the way of their plain duty.

Christmas Morning.

What a unique night! - night without parallel, in which beauty has triumphed, in which mankind, notwithstanding their delirium of slaughter, have proved the reality of their conscience.

During the intermittent bombardments a song has never ceased to rise from the whole line.

Opposite to us a most beautiful tenor was declaiming the enemy's Christmas. Much farther off, beyond the ridges, where our lines begin again, the *Marseillaise* replied. The marvellous night lavished on us her stars and meteors. Hymns, hymns, from end to end.

It was the eternal longing for harmony, the indomitable claim for order and beauty and concord.

As for me, I cherished old memories in meditating on the sweetness of the Childhood of Christ. The freshness, the dewy youthfulness of this French music, were very moving to me. I remembered the celebrated *Sommeil des Pèlerins* and the shepherds' chorus. A phrase which is sung by the Virgin thrilled me: '*Le Seigneur, pour mon fils, a béni cet asile.*' The melody rang in my ears while I was in that little house, with its neighbour in flames, and itself given over to a precarious fate.

I thought of all happinesses bestowed; I thought that you were perhaps at this moment calling down a blessing upon my abode. The sky was so lovely that it seemed to smile favourably upon all petition; but what I want strength to ask for perpetually is consistent wisdom - wisdom which, human though it may be, is none the less safe from anything that may assail it.

The sun is flooding the country and yet I write by candle-light; now and then I go out into the back gardens to see the sun. All is light, peace falling from on high upon the deserted country.

I come back to our room, where the brass of the pretty Meusian beds and the carved wood of the cupboards shine in the half-light. All these things have suffered through the rough use the soldiers put them to, but we have real comfort here. We have found table-implements and a dinner-service, and for two days running we made chocolate in a soup-tureen. Luxury!

O dear mother, if God allows me the joy of returning, what youth will this extraordinary time have brought back to me! As I wrote to my friend P——, I lead the life of a child in the midst of people so simple that even my rudimentary existence is complicated in comparison with my surroundings.

Mother dear, the length of this war tries our power of passive will, but I feel that everything is coming out as I was able to foresee. I think that these long spells of inactivity will give repose to the intellectual machine. If I ever have the happiness of once more making use of mine, it is sure to take a little time to get moving again, but with what new vigour! My last work was one of pure thought, and my ambition, which all things justify, is to give a more plastic form to my thought as it develops.

Sunday, December 27, 9 o'clock
(5th day in the first line).

It appears that the terrible position, courageously held by us on October 14th, and immediately lost by our successors, has been retaken, and 200 metres more, but at the price of a hundred casualties.

Dear mother, want of sleep robs me of all intelligence. True, one needs little of that for the general run of existence here, but I should have liked to speak to you. The only consolation is that our love needs no expression.

Very little to tell you. I was quite stupefied by the day's work yesterday, spent entirely in darkness. From my place I had only a glimpse of a pretty tree against the sky.

To-day, in the charming early morning I saw a beautiful and extremely brilliant star. I had gone to fetch some coal and water, and on the way back, when daylight had already come, that extraordinary star still persisted. My corporal, who, like me, was dodging from bush to bush back to our house, said:

'Do you know what that star is? It is the sign for the enemy's patrol to rally.'

It was true, and at first I felt outraged at this profanation of the sky, and then (apart from the ingenuity of the thing) I told myself that this star meant, for those poor creatures on the other side, that they could take the direction of safety. I felt less angry about it then. The sign had given me so much joy as a star that I decided to stick to my first impression.

Your Christmas letter came last night. Perhaps in this very hour when I am writing to you, mine of the same day is reaching you. At that time, in spite of the risk, I was enjoying all the beauty, but to-day I confess it is poisoned for me by what we hear of the last slaughter.

On the 26th we were made to remain on duty, in positions occupied only at night as a rule. Our purely defensive position was lucky that day, for we were exposed only to slight artillery fire; but on our right a regiment of our division, in one of the terrible emplacements of October 14th, received an awful punishment, of which the inconclusive result cost several hundred lives. Here in our great village, where our kind hostess knew, as we did, the victims, all is sadness.

Same day.

… Nothing attacks the soul. The torture can certainly be very great, especially the apprehension, but questions coming from the distance can be silenced by acceptation of what is close. The weather is sweet and soft, and Nature is indifferent. The dead will not spoil the spring…

And then, once the horror of the moment is over, when one sees its place taken by only the memory of those who have gone, there is a kind of sweetness in the thought of what *really exists*. In these solemn woods one realises the inanity of sepulchres and the pomp of funerals. The souls of the brave have no need of all that…

4 o'clock.

I have just finished the fourth portrait, a lieutenant in my company. He is delighted. Daylight fades. I send you my thoughts, full of cheerfulness. Hope and wisdom.

... Yesterday, after the first satisfaction of finding myself freed from manual work, I contemplated my stripes, and I felt some humiliation, because instead of the great anonymous superiority of the ordinary soldier which had put me beyond all military valuation, I had now the distinction of being a low number in military rank!

But then I felt that each time I looked at my little bits of red wool I should remember my social duty, a duty which my leaning towards individualism makes me forget only too often. So I knew I was still free to cultivate my soul, having this final effort to demand of it.

January 4, despatched on the 7th
(in a mine).

I am writing to you at the entrance to an underground passage which leads under the enemy emplacement. My little job is to look out for the safety of the sappers, who are hollowing out and supporting and consolidating an excavation about twelve metres deep already. To get to this place we have to plunge into mud up to our thighs, but during the eight hours we spend here we are sheltered by earthworks several metres thick.

I have six men, with whom I have led an existence of sleeplessness and privation for three days: this is the benefit I derive from the joyful event of my new status; but as a matter of fact I am glad to take part in these trials again.

Besides, in a few days the temporary post which I held before may be given to me altogether. Horrible weather, and to make matters worse, I burnt an absolutely new boot, and am soaking wet, like the others, but in excellent health.

Dear, I am now going to sleep a little.

DEAR MOTHER, - Here we are in a billet after seventy-two consecutive hours without sleep, living in a nameless treacly substance - rain and filth.

I have had several letters from you, dear beloved mother; the last is dated January 1. How I love them! But before speaking of them I must sleep a little.

January 7, towards mid-day.

This interrupted letter winds up at the police-station, where my section is on guard. The weather is still horrible. It's unspeakable, this derangement of our whole existence. We are under water: the walls are of mud, and the floor and ceiling too.

January 9.

... My consolations fail me in these days, on account of the weather. This horrible mess lets me see nothing whatever. I close with an ardent appeal to our love, and in the certainty of a justice higher than our own...

Dear mother, as to sending things, I am really in need of nothing. Penury now is of another kind, but courage, always! Yet is it even sure that moral effort bears any fruit?

January 13, morning
(in the trench).

I hope that when you think of me you will have in mind all those who have left everything behind: their family, their surroundings, their whole social environment; all those of whom their nearest and dearest think only in the past, saying, 'We had once a brother, who, many years ago, withdrew from this world, we know nothing of his fate.' Then I, feeling that you too have abandoned all human attachment, will walk freely in this life, closed to all ordinary relations.

I don't regret my new rank; it has brought me many troubles but a great deal of experience, and, as a matter of fact, some ameliorations.

So I want to continue to live as fully as possible in this moment, and that will be all the easier for me if I can feel that you have brought yourself to the idea that my present life cannot in any way be lost.

I did not tell you enough what pleasure the *Revues Hebdomadaires* gave me. I found some extracts from that speech on Lamartine which I am passionately fond of. Circumstances led this poet to give to his art only the lowest place. Life in general closed him round, imposing on his great heart a more serious and immediate task than that which awaited his genius.

January 15, 12.30 P.M.
(in a new billet)

We no longer have any issue whatever in sight. My only sanction is in my conscience. We must confide ourselves to an impersonal justice, independent of any human factor, and to a useful and harmonious destiny, in spite of the horrors of its form.

January 17, afternoon
(in a billet).

What shall I say to you on this strange January afternoon, when thunder is followed by snow?

Our billet provides us with many commodities, but above all with an intoxicating beauty and poetry. Imagine a lake in a park sheltered by high hills, and a castle, or, rather, a splendid country house. We lodge in the domestic offices, but I don't need any wonderful home comforts to perfect the dream-like existence that I have led here for three days. Last night we were visited by some singers. We were very far from the music that I love, but the popular and sentimental tunes were quite able to replace a finer art, because of the ardent conviction of the singer. The workman who sang these songs, which were decent, in fact moral (a rather questionable moral, perhaps, but still a moral), so put his soul into it that the timbre of his voice was altogether too moving for our hostesses. Here are the ideal people: perhaps their ideal may be said not to exist and to be purely negative, but months of suffering have taught me to honour it.

I have just seen that Charles Péguy died at the beginning of the war. How terribly French thought will have been mown down! What surpasses our understanding (and yet what is only natural) is that civilians are able to continue their normal life while we are in torment. I saw in the *Cri de Paris*, which drifted as far as here, a list of concert programmes. What a contrast! However, mother dear, the essential thing is to have known beauty in moments of grace.

The weather is frightful, but one can feel the coming of spring. At a time like this nothing can speak of individual hope, only of great general certainties.

January 19.

We have been since yesterday in our second line positions; we came to them in marvellous snow and frost. A furious sky, with charming rosy colour in it, floated over the visionary forest in the snow; the trees, limpid blue low down, brown and fretted above, the earth white.

I have received two parcels; the *Chanson de Roland* gives me infinite pleasure - particularly the Introduction, treating of the national epic and of the Mahabharata which, it seems, tells of the fight between the spirits of good and evil.

I am happy in your lovely letters. As for the sufferings which you forebode for me, they are really very tolerable.

But what we must recognise, and without shame, is that we are a *bourgeois* people. We have tasted of the honey of civilisation - poisoned honey, no doubt. But no, surely that sweetness is true, and we should not be called upon to make of our ordinary existence a preparation for violence. I know that violence may be salutary to us, especially if in the midst of it we do not lose sight of normal order and calm.

Order leads to eternal rest. Violence makes life go round. We have, for our object, order and eternal rest; but without the violence which lets loose reserves of energy, we should be too inclined to consider order as already attained. But anticipated order can only be a lethargy which retards the coming of positive order.

Our sufferings arise only from our disappointment in this delay; the coming of true order is too long for human patience. In any case, however suffering, we would rather not be doers of violence. It is as when matter in fusion solidifies too quickly and in the wrong shape: it has to be put to the fire again. This is the part violence plays in human evolution; but that salutary violence must not make us forget what our aesthetic citizenship had acquired in the way of perdurable peace and harmony. But our suffering comes precisely from the fact that we do not forget it!

January 20, morning.

Do not think that I ever deprive myself of sleep. In that matter our regiment is very fitful: one time we sleep for three days and three nights; another time, the opposite.

Now Nature gives me her support once more. The frightful spell of rain is interrupted by fine cold days. We live in the midst of beautiful frost and snow; the hard earth gives us a firm footing.

My little grade gets me some solitude. I no longer have my happy walks by night, but I have them in the day; my exemption from the hardest work gives me time to realise the beauty of things.

Yesterday, an unspeakable sunset. A filmy atmosphere, with shreds of tender colour; underneath, the blue cold of the snow.

Dear mother, it is a night of home-sickness. These familiar verses came to me in the peace:

'Mon enfant, ma soeur,
Songe à la douceur
D'aller là-bas vivre ensemble
Au pays qui te ressemble.'

Yes, Beaudelaire's *Invitation au voyage* seemed to take wing in the exquisite sky. Oh, I was far from war. Well, to return to earthly things: in coming back I nearly missed my dinner.

January 20,
evening.

Acceptation always. Adaptation to the life which goes on and on, taking no notice of our little postulations.

January 21.

We are in our first-line emplacements. The snow has followed us, but alas, the thaw too. Happily, in this emplacement we don't live in water as we do in the trenches.

Can any one describe the grace of winter trees? Did I already tell you what Anatole France says in the *Mannequin d'Osier*? He loves their delicate outlines and their intimate beauty more when they are uncovered in winter. I too love the marvellous intricate pattern of their branches against the sky.

From my post I can see our poor village, which is collapsing more and more. Each day shells are destroying it. The church is hollowed out, but its old charm remains in its ruins; it crouches so prettily between the two delicately defined hills.

We were very happy in the second line. That time of snow was really beautiful and clement. I told you yesterday about the sunset the other day. And, before that, our arrival in the marvellous woods...

January 22.

... I have sent you a few verses; I don't know what they are worth, but they reconciled me to life. And then our last billet was really wonderful in its beauty. Water running over pebbles... vast, limpid waters at the end of the park. Sleeping ponds, dreaming walks, which none of this brutality has succeeded in defiling. To-day, sun on the snow. The beauty of the snow was deeply moving, though certainly we had some bad days, days on which there was nothing for us but the wretched mud.

It seems that we won't be coming back to this pretty billet. Evidently they are making ready for something; the regularity of our winter existence has come to an end.

2 o'clock.

Splendid weather, herald of the spring, and we can make the most of it, because in this place we are allowed to put our noses out of doors.

I write badly to-day. I can only send you my love. This war is long, and I can't even speak of patience.

My only happiness is that during these five and a half months I have so often been able to tell you that everything was not ugliness...

... As for me, I have no desires left. When my trials are really hard to bear, I rest content with my own unhappiness, without facing other things.

When they become less hard, then I begin to think, to dream, and the past that is dear to me seems to have that same remote poetry which in happier days drew my thoughts to distant countries. A familiar street, or certain well-known corners, spring suddenly to my mind - just as in other days islands of dreams and legendary countries used to rise at the call of certain music and verse. But now there is no need of verse or music; the intensity of dear memories is enough.

I have not even any idea of what a new life could be; I only know that we are making life here and now.

For whom, and for what age? It hardly matters. What I do know, and what is affirmed in the very depths of my being, is that this harvest of French genius will be safely stored, and that the intellect of our race will not suffer for the deep cuts that have been made in it.

Who will say that the rough peasant, comrade of the fallen thinker, will not be the inheritor of his thoughts? No experience can falsify this magnificent intuition. The peasant's son who has witnessed the death of the young scholar or artist will perhaps take up the interrupted work, be perhaps a link in the chain of evolution which has been for a moment suspended. This is the real sacrifice: to renounce the hope of being the torch-bearer. To a child in a game it is a fine thing to carry the flag; but for a man, it is enough to know that the flag will yet be carried. And that is what every moment of great august Nature brings home to me. Every moment reassures my heart: Nature makes flags out of anything. They are more beautiful than those to which our little habits cling. And there will always be eyes to see and cherish the lessons of earth and sky.

Your dear letter of the 20th reached me last night. You must not be angry with me if occasionally, as in my letter of the 13th, I lack the very thing I am always forcing myself to acquire. But I ask you to consider what can be the thoughts of one who is young, in the fulness of productiveness, at the hour when life is flowering, if he is snatched away, and cast upon barren soil where all he has cherished fails him.

Well, after the first wrench he finds that life has not forsaken him, and sets to work upon the new ungrateful ground. The effort calls for such a concentration of energy as leaves no time for either hopes or fears. It is the constant effort at adaptation, and I manage it, except only in moments of the rebellion (quickly suppressed) of the thoughts and wishes of the past. But I need my whole strength at times for keeping down the pangs of memory and accepting what is.

I was thinking of the sad moments that you too endure, and that was why I encouraged you to an impersonal idea of our union. I know how strong you are, and how prepared for this idea. Yes, you are right, we must not meet the pain half-way. But at times it is difficult to distinguish between the real suffering that affects us, and that which is only possible or imminent.

Mind you notice that *I have perfect hope* and that I count on prevailing grace, but, caring more than anything to be an artist, I am occupied in drawing all the beauty out, in drawing out the utmost beauty, as quickly as may be, none of us knowing how much time is meted to us.

January 27, afternoon.

After two bad nights in the billet owing to the lack of straw, the third night was interrupted by our sudden departure for our emplacement in the second line.

Superb weather, frost and sun.

Great Nature begins again to enfold me, and her voice, which is now powerful again, consoles me. - But, dear, what a hole in one's existence! Yes, since my promotion I have lived through moments which, though less terrible, recalled the first days of September, but with the addition of many blessings. I accept this new life, with no forecast of the future.

January 28, in the morning sun.

The hard and splendid weather has this marvellous good - that it leaves in its great pure sky an open door for poetry. Yes, all that I told you of that beautiful time of snow came from a heart that was comforted by such triumphant beauty.

In the Reviews you send me I have read with pleasure the articles on Molière, on the English parliament, on Martainville, and on the religious questions of 1830...

Did I tell you that I learnt from the papers of the death of Hillemacher? That dear friend was killed in this terrible war.

February 1.

MY VERY DEAR MOTHER, - I have your dear letters of the 26th and 27th; they do bring new life to me.

Up till now, our first-line emplacement, which this time is in the village, has been favoured with complete calm, and I have known once more those hours of grace when Nature consoles me.

My situation has this special improvement, that the drudgery I do now is done at the instance of the general good, and no longer at the dictation of mere routine.

DEAR MOTHER, - I go on with this letter in the billet, where the great worry of accumulated work fills up the void which Melancholy would make her own.

Dark days have come upon me, and nothingness seems the end of all, whereas all that is in my being had assured me of the plenitude of the universe. Yes, devotion, not to individuals but to the social ideal of brotherhood, sustains me still. Oh, what a magnificent example is to be found in Jesus and in the poor. That righteous aristocrat, showing by His abhorrent task the infinite obligation of altruistic duty, and teaching, above all, that no return of gratitude should be demanded... To my experience of men and things I owe this tranquillity of expecting nothing from any one. Thus duty takes an abstract form, deprived of a human object.

An unspeakable sunrise to-day! Another spring draws near... I want to tell you about our three days in the first line.

Snow and frost. We went down the slopes leading to our emplacement in the village. The night was then so beautiful that it moved the heart of every soldier to see it. I could never say enough about the fine delicacy of this country. How can I explain to you the chiselled effect, allied to the dream-like mists, with the moon soaring above? For three days my night-service took me straight to the heart of this purity, this whiteness.

Tarnished gold-work of the trees. And, in spite of the mist, many colours, rose and blue.

There are hours of such beauty that those who take them to themselves can hardly die. I was well in front of the first lines, and never did I feel better protected. This morning, when I came, a pink and green sunrise over the blue and rosy snow; the open country marked with woods and covered fields; far off, the distance, in which the silvery Meuse fades away. O Beauty, in spite of all!

DEAR BELOVED MOTHER, - Your letter of the 29th has this moment come to the billet. A nameless day, a day without form, yet a day in which the spring most mysteriously begins to stir. Warm air in the lengthening days; a sudden softening, a weakening of Nature. Alas, how sweet this emotion would be if it could be felt outside this slavery, but the weakness which comes ordinarily with spring only serves here to make burdens heavier.

Dear mother, how glad I am to feel the sympathy of those who are far away. Ah, what sweetness there is!

I am delighted by the Reviews; in an admirable article on Louis Veuillot I noticed this phrase: 'O my God, take away my despair and leave my grief!' Yes, we must not misunderstand the fruitful lesson taught by grief, and if I return from this war it will most certainly be with a soul formed and enriched.

I also read with pleasure the lectures on Moliere, and in him, as elsewhere, I have viewed again the solitude in which the highest souls wander. But I owe it to my old sentimental wounds never to suffer again through the acts of others. My dearly loved mother, I will write to you better to-morrow.

February 4.

Last night, on coming back to the barn, drunkenness, quarrels, cries, songs and yells. Such is life!... But when morning came and the wakening from sleep still brought me memories of this, I got up before the time, and found outside a friendly moon, and the great night taking wing, and a dawn which had pity on me. The blessed spring day gilds everything and scatters its promises and hopes.

Dear, I was reflecting on Tolstoi's title, *War and Peace*. I used to think that he wanted to express the antithesis of these two states, but now I ask myself if he did not connect these two contraries in one and the same folly - if the fortunes of humanity, whether at war or at peace, were not equally a burden to his mind. By all means let us keep faithful to our efforts to be good; but in spite of ourselves we take this precept a little in the sense of the placards: 'Be good to animals.' How hard it is, in the midst of daily duties, to keep guard upon oneself.

February 5.

A sleepless night. Hateful return to the barn. Such a fearful row that the corporals had to complain. Punishments.

In the morning, on the march, and, in order to rest us, work to-night!

February 6.

MY DEAR BELOVED MOTHER, - After the sleepless night in our billet, we had to supply a working-party all the following night. So I have been sleeping up till the very moment of writing to you. Sleep and Night are refuges which give life still one attraction.

Mother dear, I am living over again the lovely legend of Sarpedon; and that exquisite flower of Greek poetry really gives me comfort. If you will read this passage of the *Iliad* in my beautiful translation by Lecomte de l'Isle, you will see that Zeus utters in regard to destiny certain words in which the divine and the eternal shine out as nobly as in the Christian Passion. He suffers, and his fatherly heart undergoes a long battle, but finally he permits his son to die, and Hypnos and Thanatos are sent to gather up the beloved remains.

Hypnos - that is Sleep. To think that I should come to that, I for whom every waking hour was a waking joy, I for whom every moment of action was a thrill of pride. I catch myself longing for the escape of Sleep from the tumult that besets me. But the splendid Greek optimism shines out as in those vases at the Louvre. By the two, Hypnos and Thanatos, Sarpedon is lifted to a life beyond his human death; and assuredly Sleep and Death do wonderfully magnify and continue our mortal fate.

Thanatos - that is a mystery, and it is a terror only because the urgency of our transitory desires makes us misconceive the mystery. But read over again the great peaceful words of Maeterlinck in his book on death, words ringing with compassion for our fears in the tremendous passage of mortality.

February 7.

MOST DEAR AND MOST BELOVED, - I have your splendid letter of the first. Please don't hesitate to write what you think I would call mere chatter. Your love and the absolute identity of our two hearts appear in all your letters. And that is all I really care for. Yet they tell me a thousand things that interest me too.

We are living through hours of heavy labour. My rank gives me respite now and then; but for the men it means five nights at a time without sleep, and this repeatedly.

February 9.

Another breathing-space in which, almost at my last gasp, I get a brief peace. The little reviving breath comes again. I have had the good luck to be appointed corporal on guard in delightful quarters, where I am in command. Perfect spring weather. And what can I say of this Nature? Never before have I so fully felt her amplitude of life. Hours and seasons following one another surely, infallibly, unalterably, in unchanging unity; the looker-on has a glimpse of the immensity of the force that first set them afoot.

I had often known the delight of watching the nearer coming of a season, but it had not before been given to me to live in that delight moment by moment. It is so that one learns, without the help of any kind of science, a certain intuition, vague perhaps, but altogether indisputable, of the Absolute. There was a man of science, possibly a great one, who declared that he had not discovered God under his scalpel. What a shocking mistake for an able mind to make! Where was the need of a scalpel, when the joy and the thrill of our senses are all-sufficient to convince us of the purpose commanding our whole evolution? The poet watches the coming of the seasons as it were great ships that will, he knows, set sail again. At times the storm may delay them, but at their next coming they will bring with them the rich fragrance of the unknown coasts. A season coming again to our own shores seems to bring us delights which it has learnt by long travel.

Ah, dearest mother, if one could have again a retreat for the soul! O solitude, for those worthy to possess it! How seldom is it inviolate!

February 11.

It may possibly be a great intended privilege for our generation to be a witness of these horrors, but what a terrible price to pay! Well, faith, eternal faith, is over all. Faith in an evolution, an Order, beyond our human patience.

February 11
(2nd day in the front line).

In such hours as these one must perforce take refuge in the extra-human principle of sacrifice; it is impossible for mere humanity to go further.

Let go all poor human hope. Seek something beyond; perhaps you have already found it. As for me, I feel myself to be unworthy in such days to be anything more than a memory. I picked some flowers in the mud. Keep them in remembrance of me.

5 o'clock.

Courage through all, courage in spite of all.

February 13
(4th day in the front line).

BELOVED, - After the days of tears and of rebellion of the heart that have so shaken me, I pull myself together again to say 'Thy will be done.' So, according to the power and the measure of my faculties, I would be he who to the very end never despaired of his share in the building of the Temple. I would be the workman who, knowing full well that his scaffolding will give way and who has no hope of safety, goes on with his stone-carving of decoration on the cathedral front. Decoration. I am not one who will ever be able to lift the blocks of stone. But there are others for that job. Yes, I am getting back into a little quiet thinking. The equable tranquillity I had hoped for is not yet mine; but I have occasional glimpses of that region of peace and light in which all things, even our love, is renewed and transfigured.

I am now at the foot of a peaked hill where Nature has brought the loveliest lines of design together. Man is hunting man, and in a moment they will be locked in fight. Meanwhile the lark is rising.

Even as I write, a strange serenity possesses me. Something - extraordinary comfort. Be it a human quality, be it a revelation from on high. All around me men are asleep.

February 14
(5th day in the front line).

All is movement about us; we too are afoot. Even as the inevitable takes shape, peace revisits my heart at last. My beloved country is defiled by these detestable preparations of battle; the silence is rent by the preliminary gun-fire; man succeeds for a time in cancelling all the beauty of the world. But I think it will even yet find a place of refuge. For twenty-four hours now I have been my own self.

Dear mother, I was wrong to think so much of my 'tower of ivory.' What we too often take for a tower of ivory is nothing more than an old cheese where a hermit rat has made his house.

Rather, may a better spirit move me to gratitude for the salutary shocks that tossed me out of too pleasant a place of peace; let us be thankful for the dispensation which, during certain hours - hours far apart but never to be forgotten - made a man of me.

No, no, I will not mourn over my dead youth. It led me by steep and devious ways to the tablelands where the mists that hung over intelligence are no more.

February 16.

In these latter days I have passed through certain hours, made decisive hours for me by the visibility of great and universal problems. We have now been for five days in the front line, with exceedingly hard work, hampered by the terrible mud. As our days have followed each other, and as my own struggle against the frightful sadness of my soul continued, the military situation was growing more tense, and the preparation for action was pushing on. Then came the announcement of the order of attack. There was only a day left - perhaps two days. It was then I wrote you two letters, I think those of the 13th and 14th; and really, as I was writing, I had within my heart such a plenitude of conviction, such a sweetness of feeling, as give incontrovertible assurance of the reality of the beautiful and the good. The bombardment of our position was violent; but nothing that man can do is able to stifle or silence what Nature has to say to the human soul.

One night, between the 14th and the 15th, we were placed in trenches that were raked by machine-guns. Our men were so exhausted that they were obliged to give place to another battalion. We were waiting in the wet and the cold of night when suddenly the notice came that we were relieved. We could not tell why. But we are here again in this village, where the men deluge their poor hearts with wine. I am in the midst of them.

Dear mother, if there is one thing absolute in human feeling, it is pain. I had lived hitherto in the contemplation of the interesting relations of different emotions, losing sight of the price, the intrinsic value, of life itself. But now I know what is essential life. It is that which clears the soul's way to the Absolute. But I suffered less in that time of waiting than I am suffering now from certain companionships.

February 16, 9 o'clock.

DEAR BELOVED MOTHER, - I was at dinner when they came to tell me we were off. I knew it would be so; the counter-orders that put off the attack cost us the march of forty kilometres in addition to the fatigues we had to undergo in the first line. As we were leaving our sector I noticed the arrival of such a quantity of artillery that I knew well enough the pause was at an end. But the soul has its own peace. It is frosty weather, with a sky full of stars.

February 19
(sent off in the full swing of battle).

One word only. We are in the hands of God. Never, never, have we so needed the wisdom of confidence. Death prevails, but it does not reign. Life is still noble. Friends of mine killed and wounded yesterday and the day before. Dearest, our messengers may be greatly delayed.

We are in billets after the great battle. And this time I saw it all. I did my duty; I knew that by the feeling of my men for me. But the best are dead. Bitter loss. This heroic regiment. We gained our object. Will write at more length.

February 22
(1st day in billet).

DEAR BELOVED MOTHER, - I will tell you about the goodness of God, and the horror of these things. The heaviness of heart that weighed me down this month and a half past was for the coming anguish to be undergone in these last twenty days.

We reached the scene of action on the 17th. The preparation ceased to interest me; I was all expectation of the event. It broke out at three o'clock: the explosion of seven mines under the enemy's trenches. It was like a distant thunder. Next, five hundred guns created the hell into which we leapt.

Night was coming on when we established ourselves in the positions we had taken. All that night I was actively at work for the security of our men, who had not suffered much. I had to cover great tracts, over which were scattered the wounded and the dead of both sides. My heart yearned over them, but I had nothing better than words to give them. In the morning we were driven, with serious loss, back to our previous positions, but in the evening we attacked again; we retook our whole advance; here again I did my duty. In my advance I got the sword of an officer who surrendered; after that I placed my men for guarding our ground. The captain ordered me to his side, and I gave him the plan of our position. He was telling me of his decision to have me mentioned, when he was killed before my eyes.

Briefly, under the frightful fire of those three days, I organised and kept going the work of supplying cartridges; in this job five of my men were wounded. Our losses are terrible; those of the enemy greater still. You cannot imagine, beloved mother, what man will do against man. For five days my shoes have been slippery with human brains, I have walked among lungs, among entrails. The men eat, what little they have to eat, at the side of the dead. Our regiment was heroic; we have no officers left. They all died as brave men. Two good friends - one of them a fine model of my own for one of my last pictures - are killed. That was one of the terrible incidents of the evening. A white body, splendid under the moon! I lay down near him. The beauty of things awoke again for me.

At last, after five days of horror that lost us twelve hundred men, we were ordered back from the scene of abomination.

The regiment has been mentioned in despatches.

Dear mother, how shall I ever speak of the unspeakable things I have had to see? But how shall I ever tell of the certainties this tempest has made clear to me? Duty; effort.

February 23.

DEAREST BELOVED MOTHER, - A second day in billets. To-morrow we go to the front. Darling, I can't write to-day. Let us draw ever nearer to the eternal, let us remain devoted to our duty. I know how your thoughts fly to meet mine, and I turn mine towards the happiness of wisdom. Let us take courage; let me be brave among these young dead men, and be you brave in readiness. God is over us.

February 26
(a splendid afternoon).

DEAR MOTHER, - Here we are again upon the battlefield. We have climbed the hill from which it would be better to praise the glory of God than to condemn the horrors of men. Innumerable dead at the setting-out of our march; but they grow fewer, leaving here and there some poor stray body, the colour of clay - a painful encounter. Our losses are what are called 'serious' in despatches.

At all events I can assure you that our men are admirable and their resignation is heroic. All deplore this infamous war, but nearly all feel that the fulfilment of a hideous duty is the one only thing that justifies the horrible necessity of living at such a time as this.

Dear mother, I cannot write more. The plain is settling to sleep under colours of violet and rose. How can things be so horrible?

February 28
(in a billet).

DEAR BELOVED MOTHER, AND DEAR BELOVED GRANDMOTHER, - I am writing to you, having just struggled out of a most appalling nightmare, and out of Dantesque scenes that I have lived through. Things that Gustave Dore had the courage to picture through the text of the *Divina Commedia* have come to pass, with all the variety and circumstance of fact. In the midst of labours that happily tend to deaden one's feelings, I have been able to gather the better fruits of pain.

On the 24th, in the evening, we returned to our positions, from which the more hideous of the traces of battle had been partly removed. Only a few places were still scattered with fragments of men that were taking on the semblance of that clay to which they were returning. The weather was fine and cold, and the heights we had gained brought us into the very sky. The immensities appeared only as lights: the higher light, a brilliance of stars; the lower light, a glow of fires. The frightful bombardment with which the Germans overwhelm us is really a waste of fireworks.

I lay in a dug-out from which I could follow the moon, and watch for daybreak. Now and again a shell crumbled the soil about me, and deafened me; then silence came again upon the frozen earth. I have paid the price, I have paid dearly, but I have had moments of solitude that were full of God.

I really think I have tried to adapt myself to my work, for, as I told you, I am proposed for the rank of sergeant and for mention in despatches. Ah, but, dearest mother, this war is long, too long for men who had something else to do in the world! What you tell me of the kind feeling there is for me in Paris gives me pleasure; but - am I not to be brought out of this for a better kind of usefulness? Why am I so sacrificed, when so many others, not my equals, are spared? Yet I had something worth doing to do in the world. Well, if God does not intend to take away this cup from me, His will be done.

March 3
(in a billet).

This is the fourth day of rest, for me almost a holiday time. Rather a sad holiday, I own; it reminds me of certain visits to Marlotte. These days have been spent in attempts to recover from physical fatigue and moral weariness, and in the filling up of vacant hours. Still, a kind of holiday, a halt rather, giving one time to arrange one's impressions, so long confused by the violence of action.

I have been stupefied by the noise of the shells. Think - from the French side alone forty thousand have passed over our heads, and from the German side about as many, with this difference, that the enemy shells burst right upon us. For my own part, I was buried by three 305 shells at once, to say nothing of the innumerable shrapnel going off close by. You may gather that my brain was a good deal shaken. And now I am reading. I have just read in a magazine an article on three new novels, and that reading relieved many of the cares of battle.

I have received a most beautiful letter from André, who must be a neighbour of mine out here. He thinks as I do about our dreadful war literature. What does flourish is a faculty of musical improvisation. All last night I heard the loveliest symphonies, fully orchestral; and I am bound to say that they owed their best to the great music that is Germany's.

After my experiences I must really let myself go a little in the pleasure of this furtive sun of March.

March 5 (6th day in billets).

I wish I could recover in myself the extreme sensibilities I felt before the fiery trial, so that I might describe for you the colours and the aspects of the drama we have passed through. But just now I am in a state of numbness, pleasant enough in itself, yet apt to hinder my vision of things present and my forecasts of things to come. I have to make an effort to keep hold of eternal and essential things; perhaps I shall succeed in time.

And yet certain sights on the wasted field of war had so noble a lesson, a teaching so persuasive, that I should love to share with you the great certainties of those days. How harmonious is death within the natural soil, how admirable is the manner of man's return to the substance of his mother earth, compared with the poverty of funeral ceremonial! Yesterday I thought of those poor dead as forsaken things. But I had been present at the burial of an officer, and it seems to me that Nature is more compassionate than man. Yes indeed, the soldier's death is close to natural things. It is a frank horror, a horror that does not attempt to cheat the law of violence. I often passed close to bodies that were gradually passing into the clay, and their change seemed more comforting than the cold and unchanging aspect of the tombs of town cemeteries. From our life in the open we have gained a freedom of conception, an amplitude of thought and of habit, which will for ever make cities horrible and artificial to those who survive the war.

Dear mother, I write but ill of things that I have greatly felt. Let us seek refuge in the peace of spring and in the treasure of the present moment.

DEAR BELOVED MOTHER, - I am filling up the idleness of this morning. I am rejoicing in the clear waters of the Meuse that give life to dales and gardens. The play of the current over weeds and pebbles makes a soothing sight for my tired eyes, and expresses the calm life of this big village that is sheltered by the Meuse hills. The church here is thronged with soldiers who possess, as I do, a definite intuition of the Ideal, but who seek it by more stated and less immediate means.

I am to board for a fortnight in the house in which, nearly two months ago, our joyous company used to meet. To-day I have seen the tears of these same friends, weeping to hear of the wounded and the dead.

I received your sleeping-sack, which is quite right. I am worried with rheumatism, which has spoilt many of my nights in billets these two months past.

Darling mother, here is a calm in the noise of that barrack-life which must now be ours. As there are none here but non-commissioned officers, they are all ordered to hard jobs, and I shall renew my acquaintance with brooms and burdens. We have been warned; we shall have to work with our hands. And so we learn to direct others.

March 7 (another letter).

Soft weather after rain. Bells in the evening; flowing waters singing under the bridges; trees settling to sleep.

March 11.

DARLING MOTHER, - I have nothing to say about my life, which is filled up with manual labour. At moments perhaps some image appears, some memory rises. I have just read a fine article by Renan on the origins of the Bible. I found it in a *Revue des Deux Mondes* of 1886. If later I can remember something of it, I may be able to put my very scattered notions on that matter into better order.

I feel as though I were recovering from typhoid fever. What I chiefly enjoy is water; the running and the sleeping waters of the Meuse. The springs play on weeds and pebbles. The ponds lie quiet under great trees. Streams and waterfalls. On the steep hillsides the snow looks brilliant and visionary. I live in all these things without forms of words. And I am rather ashamed to be vegetating, though I think all must pass through this phase, just removed from the hell of the front. I eat, and when my horrid rheumatism allows, I sleep.

Don't be angry with my inferiority. I feel as though my armour had been taken off. Well, I can't help it.

5 o'clock.

I am a good deal tired by drill. But the fine air of the Meuse keeps me in health. Dear mother, I wish I might always seek all that is noble and good. I wish I might always feel within myself the inspiration that urges towards the true treasures of life. But alas! just now I have a mind of lead.

March 14, Sunday morning, in the Sabbath peace.

DEAREST MOTHER, - Your good, life-giving letters have come at last, after my long privation, the price I paid for my enjoyment of rest. The pretty town is waking in the haze of the river, the waters hurry over their clean stones. All things have that look of moderation and charming finish that is characteristic of this part of the country.

I read a little, but I am so overtired by the physical exertion to which we are compelled, that I fall asleep on the instant. We are digging trenches and trenches.

Dear mother, to go back to those wonderful times of the end of February, I must repeat that my memory of them is something like that of an experiment in science. I had conceived violence under a theoretic formula; I had divined its part in the worlds. But I had not yet witnessed its actual practice, except in infinitely small examples. And now at last violence was displayed before me on such a scale that my whole faculty of receptiveness was called upon to face it. Well, it was interesting; and I may tell you that I never relaxed from my attitude of cool and impersonal watchfulness. What I had kept about me of my own individuality was a certain visual perceptiveness that caused me to register the setting of things, a setting that dramatised itself as 'artistically' as in any stage-management. During all those minutes I never relaxed in my resolve to see 'how it was.'

I was very happy to find that the 'intoxication of slaughter' never had any possession of me. I hope it will always be so. Unfortunately, contact with the German race has for ever spoilt my opinion of those people. I cannot quite succeed in quelling a sensibility and a humanitarianism that I know to be misplaced, and that would make me the dupe of a treacherous enemy; but I have come to tolerate things which I had held in abomination as the very negation of life.

I have seen the French soldier fight. He is terrible in action, and after action magnanimous. That is the phrase. It is a very common commonplace; our greatest writers and the humblest of our schoolboys have trotted it out alike; and now my decadent ex-intellectualism finds nothing better to say at the sight of the soul of the Frenchman.

To Madame de L.

March 14, 1915.

My mother has told me of the new trial that has just come upon you. Truly life is crushing for some souls. I know your fortitude, and I know that you are only too well used to sorrow; but how much I wish that you had been spared this blow! My mother had written to me of the lack of any news of Colonel B., and she was anxious. It is the grief of those dear to us that troubles us out here. But there is in the sight of a soldier's death a lesson of greatness and of immortality that arms our hearts; and our desire is that our beloved ones might share it with us. Be sure that the Colonel's example will bear magnificent fruit. I know, for I have seen it, what heroism transfigures the soldier whose leader has fallen.

As for myself, the time has been rife with tragedies; throughout I have tried to do my duty.

I saw all my superior officers killed, and the whole regiment decimated. There can be no more human hope for those who are cast into this furnace. I place myself in the hands of God, asking of Him that He would keep me in such a state of heart and soul as may enable me to enjoy and love in His creation all the beauty that man has not yet denied and concealed.

All else has lost proportion in my life.

March 15
(a post-card).

DEAR BELOVED MOTHER, - I suppose that by now you know my good fortune in getting this platoon. Whatever God intends for me, this halt has given me the opportunity of regaining possession of myself, and of preparing myself to accept whatever may befall me. I send you my love and the union of our hearts in the face of fate.

March 17.

A charming morning. A white sun swathing itself in mist, the fine outlines of trees on the heights, and the great spaces in light. It is a pause full of good luck. The other day, reading an old *Revue des Deux Mondes* of 1880, I came upon an excellent article as one might come upon a noble palace with vaulted roof and decorated walls. It was on Egypt, and was signed George Perrot.

Yesterday my battalion left these billets. I am obliged to stay behind for my instruction as sergeant. How thankful I am for this respite, laborious as it is, that gives me a chance of recovering what I care for most - a clear mind, and a heart open to the spirit of Nature.

I forgot to tell you that a day or two ago, during the storm, I saw the cranes coming home towards evening. A lull in the weather allowed me to hear their cry. To think how long it is since I saw them take flight from here! It was at the beginning of the winter, and they left everything the sadder for their going. And now it was for me like the coming of the dove to the ark; not that I deceived myself as to the dangers that had not ceased, but that these ambassadors of the air brought me a visible assurance of the universal peace beyond our human strife.

And yesterday the wild geese made for the north. They flew in various order, tracing regular formations in the sky; and then they disappeared over the horizon like a floating ribbon.

I am much gratified by M.C.'s appreciation. I always had a love of letters, even as a child, and I am only sorry that the break in my education, brought about by myself, leaves so many blanks. I keep, however, throughout all changes and chances, the faculty of gleaning to right and left some fallen grain. Of course, as I leave out the future, I say nothing of my wish to be introduced to him in happier times - that is out of our department just now.

I have written to Madame L. It is the last blow for her. The fate of some of us is as it were a medal on which are struck the image and superscription of sorrow. Adversity has worked so well that there is no room for any symbol of joy. But I think that this dedication of a life to grief is not unaccompanied by a secret compensation in the conviction that misfortune is at last complete; it is something to reach the high-water mark of the waters of sorrow. The fate of such sufferers seems to me to be an outpost showing others whence tribulation approaches.

Day by day a new crop is raised in the little military burial-ground here. And, over all, the triumphant spring.

March 20.

Our holiday is coming to an end in sweetness, while all is tumult and carnage not far off. I think the regiment has had a long march.

March 20.

DEAR BELOVED MOTHER, - After so many graces granted me, I ought to have more confidence, and I intend to do my best to give myself wholly into the hands of God; but these are hard times. I have just heard of the death, among many others, of the friend whose bed I shared in our billet. He had just been appointed Second Lieutenant. Mother dear: Love. That is the only human feeling we may cherish now.

March 21.

DEAR GRANDMOTHER, - As the day of trial draws near I send you all my love. I can do no more. We are probably called upon to make such a sacrifice as forbids us to dwell upon our ties. Let us pray that the certitude of Goodness and Beauty may not fail us when we suffer.

March 21, Sunday, with lovely sunshine.

DEAR BELOVED MOTHER, - I think that we may be kept here one day more, and that we shall leave on Tuesday. I don't know where I shall rejoin my battalion, or in what state I shall find it, for the action seems to be violent and long. Rumours are very contradictory as to our gains. But all agree as to the large number of casualties. We can hear a tremendous cannonade, and the good weather no doubt induces the command on both sides to move.

I should have wished to say many things about the noble Nature that surrounds us with its glory, but my thoughts are gone on in advance, there where the sun does not see men gathered together to honour him, but shines only upon their hatred, and where the moon, too, looks upon treachery and anguish.

The other day, overlooking this great prospect of earth welcoming the spring, I remembered the joy I once had to be a man. And now to be a man——

Our neighbour regiment, that of R.L., has returned with a few of its companies reduced to some two-score men.

I dare not now speak of hope. The grace for which one may still pray is a complete sense of what beauty the passing hour can still yield us. It is a new manner of 'living one's life' that literature had not foreseen.

Dear Grandmother, how well your tenderness has served to keep me up in my time of trial.

March 22.

A splendid sun; looking on it one is amazed to see the world at war. Spring has come in triumph. It has surprised mankind in the act of hatred, in the act of outrage upon creation. The despatches tell us little, fortunately, of what is happening.

Being now these twenty-one days away from the front, I find it difficult to re-accustom myself to the thought of the monstrous things going on there. Indeed, dear mother, I know that your life and mine have had but one object, one aim, and that even in the time we are passing through, we have never lost sight of it, but have constantly tried to draw nearer.

Therefore our lives may not have been altogether useless. This is the only thought to comfort an ambitious soul - to forecast the influence and the consequences of its acts.

I believe that if longer life had been granted me I should never have relaxed in my purpose. Having no certainty but that of the present, I have tried to put myself to the best use.

Here I am living this life in the earth again. I found the very hole that I left last month. Nothing has been done while I was away; a formidable attack was attempted, but it failed. The regiments ordered to engage had neither our dash nor our perfect steadiness under fire. They succeeded only in getting themselves cut to pieces, and in bringing upon us the most atrocious bombardment that ever was. It seems the action before this was nothing to be compared with it. My company lost a great many men by the aerial bombs. These projectiles measure a metre in height and twenty-seven centimetres in diameter; they describe a high curve, and fall vertically, exploding in the narrowest passages. We are several metres deep underground. Pleasant weather. At night we go to the surface for our hard work.

Dearest, I wanted to say a heap of things about our joys, but some of them are best left quiet, unawakened. All coarse, common pleasure would frighten them away - they might die.

I am writing again after a sleep. We get all the sleep we can in our dug-outs.

I had a pile of thoughts that fatigue prevents my putting in order; but I remember that I evoked Beethoven. I am now precisely at the age he had reached when disaster came upon him; and I admired his great example, his energies at work in spite of suffering. The impediment must have seemed to him as grave as what is before me seems to us; but he conquered. To my mind Beethoven is the most magnificent of human translations of the creative Power.

I am writing badly, for I am still asleep.

How easy, how kind were all the circumstances of my return! I left the house alone, but passing a battery of artillery I was accosted by the non-commissioned officers with offers of the most friendly hospitality. The artillery are devoted to the Tenth, for we defend them; and as the good fellows are not even exposed to the rain they pity us exceedingly.

I must close abruptly, loving you for your courage that so sustains me. Whatever happens, I have recovered joy. The night I came was so lovely!

DEARLY BELOVED MOTHER, - Nothing new in our position; the organising goes on. Interesting but not easy work. The fine weather prospers it. Now and again our pickaxes come upon a poor dead man whom the war harasses even in his grave.

March 28
(on the heights; a grey Sunday; weather broken by yesterday's
bombardment).

We are again in full fight. A great attack from our side has repeated the carnage of last week. My company, which was cut up in the last assault, was spared this time; we had nothing to do but occupy a sector of the defence. So we got only the splashes of the fighting.

On the loveliest Saturday of this spring I had a distant view of the battle; I saw the crawling beast that a battalion looks like, twisting as it advances under the smoke of the guns. The *chasseurs à pied* go forward in spite of the machine-guns and of the bombardment, French and German. These fine fellows did what they had to do in spite of all, and have made amends for the check we had last week when our attack was a failure.

For a month past I have been living Raffet's lithographs, with this difference, that in his time one could be an eyewitness in comparative safety at the distance where I stood, for the guns of those days did not shoot far. But I saw fine things in that great plain beneath our heights; a hundred thousand fires of bursting shells. And the *chasseurs* climbing, climbing.

DEAR MOTHER, - Radiant weather rose this morning. I have been a long way over our sector, and now the bombardment begins again, and grows.

And still I turn my thoughts to hope. Whatever happens, I pray for wisdom for you and for me.

Dearest, I feel at times how easy it would be to turn again to those pursuits that were once the charm and the interest of my life. At times I catch myself, in this lovely spring, so bent upon painting that I could mourn because I paint no more. But I compel myself to master all the resources of my will and to keep them to the difficult straits of this life.

April 1.

A sun that lays bare the lovely youth of the spring. The stream of the Meuse runs through this rich and comely village, which the echoes of the cannonade reach only as a dull thud, their meaning lost.

We have had to change again, as the reinforcements are arriving in such numbers that our places are wanted; and it is always our regiment that has to turn out.

But to-day all is freshness and light. The great rich plain that is edged by the Meuse uplands has its distance all invested in the tenderest silver tones.

I am pleased with Gabrielle's letter; it shows me what things will be laid upon the heart of France when these events are at an end. A touching letter from Pierre, cured at last of his terrible wound. A splendid letter from Grandmother. How she longs for our meeting again! I cannot speak of it.

*   *   *   *   *

I finish this letter by the waterside, recalling with delight the joys I used to have in painting. Before me are the sparkling rays of spring.

Only a word from the second line. We are in the spring woods. Sun and rain at play in the sky. Courage through all.

I wish I had written you better letters in these days, every minute of which has been sweet to me, even when we were in the front line. But I confess that I was satisfied just to let myself live in the beauty of the days, serene days in spite of the clamours of war. We know nothing of what is to happen. But there is more movement - coming and going. Shall we have to bear the shock again?

Think what it was for us when we were last in the front line, to have to spend whole days in the dug-out that the odious bombardment had compelled us to hollow out of the hillside ten metres deep. There, in complete darkness, night was awaited for the chance to get out. But once my fellow non-commissioned officers and I began humming the nine symphonies of Beethoven. I cannot tell what thrill woke those notes within us. They seemed to kindle great lights in the cave. We forgot the Chinese torture of being unable to lie, or sit, or stand.

The life of a sergeant in billets is really quite pleasant. But I take no advantage. As to the front, I hope Providence will give me strength of heart to do my duty there to the very end. A good friend of mine, who was my section-chief, has been appointed adjutant to our company. This is all trivial enough; but, dearest, I am in a rather feeble state; I was not well after the events of last month. So I let myself glide over the gentle slopes of my life. Suppose one comes to skirt a precipice? May Providence keep us away from the edge!

April 4.

DARLING MOTHER, - A time of anxious waiting, big with the menace of near things. Meanwhile, however, idleness and quiet. I am not able to think, and I give myself up to my fate. Beloved, don't find fault with me if for a month past I have been below the mark. Love me, and tell our friends to love me.

Did you get my photograph? It was taken at the fortunate time of our position here, when we were having peaceful days, with no immediate enemy except the cold. A few days later I was made corporal, and my life became hard enough, burdened with very ungrateful labours. After that, the storm; and the lights of that storm are still bright in my life.

April 4, evening of Easter Sunday.

DEAR MOTHER, - We are again in the immediate care of God. At two o'clock we march towards the storm. Beloved, I think of you, I think of you both. I love you, and I entrust the three of us to the Providence of God. May everything that happens find us ready! In the full power of my soul, I pray for this, on your behalf, on mine: hope through all; but, before all else, Wisdom and Love.

I kiss you, without more words. All my mind is now set upon the hard work to be done.

April 5, 1 o'clock A.M.

DEAR MOTHER AND DEAR GRANDMOTHER, - We are off. Courage. Wisdom and Love. Perhaps all this is ordained for the good of all. I can but send you my whole love. My life is lived in you alone.

April 5, towards noon.

DEAR MOTHER, - We are now to be put to the proof. Up to this moment there has been no sign that mercy was failing us. It is for us to strive to deserve it. This afternoon we shall need all our resolution, and we shall have to call upon the supreme Wisdom for help.

Dear beloved Mother, dear Grandmother, I wish I could still have the delight of getting your letters. Let us pray that we may be strengthened even in what is before us now.

Dear Darling, once more all my love for you both.

YOUR SON.

April 6, noon.

DEAR BELOVED MOTHER, - It is mid-day, and we are at the forward position, in readiness. I send you my whole love. Whatever comes to pass, life has had its beauty.

It was in the fight of this day, April 6, that the writer of these letters disappeared.